my **revision** notes

AS Edexcel History
THE EXPERIENCE OF WARFARE

Barbara Warnock

Series editors:
Robin Bunce
Laura Gallagher

**HODDER
EDUCATION**
AN HACHETTE UK COMPANY

Text credits

Correlli Barnett, *Britain and her Army 1509–1970 – a military, political and social survey* (Allen Lane, 1970); **Sydney Bond**, quoted in Richard Van Emden and Steve Humphries, *All Quiet on the Home Front* (Headline, 2003); **Joanna Bourke**, *Dismembering the Male* (Reaktion Books, 1996); **Sydney Checkland**, *British Public Policy 1776–1939* (Cambridge University Press, 1983); **Winston S. Churchill**, quoted in Tabitha Jackson, *The Boer War* (Channel 4 Books, 1999); **Vic Cole**, quoted in Richard Van Emden and Steve Humphries, *All Quiet On the Home Front* (Headline, 2003); **George Coppard**, *With a Machine Gun to Cambrai – the tale of a young Tommy in Kitchener's Army 1914–1918* (HMSO, 1969); **Gordon Corrigan**, *Mud, Blood and Poppycock* (Cassell, 2003), reproduced by permission of The Orion Publishing Group, London; **Saul David**, *The Homicidal Earl: The Life of Lord Cardigan* (Little, Brown, 1997); **Jack Davis**, quoted in Richard Van Emden and Steve Humphries, *All Quiet on the Home Front* (Headline, 2003); **Richard Van Emden and Steve Humphries**, *All Quiet on the Home Front* (Headline, 2003); **Orlando Figes**, *Crimea – The Last Crusade* (Allen Lane, 2011); **Philip Gibbs**, quoted in Gerard De Groot, *Blighty – British Society in the Era of the Great War* (Longman, 1996); **Gerard De Groot**, *Blighty – Britain in the Era of the Great War* (Longman, 1996) reproduced by permission of the author; **Amelia Harris**, quoted in Richard Van Emden and Steve Humphries, *All Quiet on the Home Front* (Headline, 2003); **J. F. C. Harrison**, *Late Victorian Britain* (Routledge, 1990); **Basil Liddell Hart**, quoted in John Mearsheimer, *Liddell Hart and the weight of history* (Brassey's Defence, 1988); **Gwen Herford**, quoted in Rosemary Rees and Geoffrey Stewart, *The Experience of Warfare in Britain 1854–1929* (Heinemann, 2008); **J. L. Jack**, *General Jack's Diary 1914–1918: The Trench Diary of Brigadier-General J. L. Jack DSO*, edited by John Terraine (Eyre & Spottiswoode, 1964), reproduced by permission of Peters Fraser & Dunlop (www.petersfraserdunlop.com) on behalf of the Estate of John Terraine; **Denis Judd and Keith Surridge**, *The Boer War* (John Murray, 2003); **Norman Lowe**, *Mastering World History* (Macmillan, 1982); **General von Ludendorff**, *My War Memories 1914–1918* (Hutchinson, 1919); **Major-General Sir W.P. MacPherson**, quoted in Joanna Bourke, *Dismembering the Male* (Reaktion Books, 1996); **Charlie Miles**, quoted in Trevor Wilson, *The Myriad Faces of War* (Polity, 1989); **Bill Moore**, quoted in Richard Van Emden and Steve Humphries, *All Quiet on the Home Front* (Headline, 2003); **John Nettleton**, *The Anger of Guns: An Infantry Officer on the Western Front* (Kimber, 1979); **Colonel Walter Norris Nicholson**, quoted in Joanna Bourke, *Dismembering the Male* (Reaktion Books, 1996); **Thomas Pakenham**, *The Boer War* (Cardinal, 1991); **Len Payne**, quoted in Rosemary Rees and Geoffrey Stewart, *The Experience of Warfare in Britain 1854–1929* (Heinemann, 2008); **Clive Ponting**, *The Crimean War – The Truth Behind the Myth* (Chatto & Windus, 2004), reprinted by permission of The Random House Group Ltd; **Robin Prior and Trevor Wilson**, *The Somme* (Yale University Press, 2006); **Rosemary Rees and Geoffrey Stewart**, *The Experience of Warfare in Britain* (Heinemann, 2008); **Deneys Reitz**, *Commando: A Boer Journal of the Boer War* (Faber & Faber, 1929); **Peter Rowland**, *Lloyd George* (Barrie & Jenkins, 1975); **Mary Seacole**, *The Wonderful Adventures of Mrs Seacole in Many Lands* (1857); **John A. Shepherd**, *The Crimean Doctors – a History of the British Medical Services in the Crimean War* (Liverpool University Press, 1991); **Hew Strachan**, *The First World War – a new illustrated history* (Simon & Schuster, 2003); **Arthur Surfleet**, quoted in Trevor Wilson, *The Myriad Faces of War* (Polity, 1989); **John Sweetman**, *War and Administration – the Significance of the Crimean War for the British Army* (Scottish Academic Press, 1984); **Alfred Tennyson**, 'The Charge of the Light Brigade' (1854); **Walker Henderson Thomson**, quoted in Tabitha Jackson, *The Boer War* (Channel 4 Books, 1999); **Rina Viljoen**, quoted in Tabitha Jackson, *The Boer War* (Channel 4 Books, 1999); **Minnie Way**, quoted in Tabitha Jackson, *The Boer War* (Channel 4 Books, 1999); **Trevor Wilson**, *The Myriad Faces of War* (Polity, 1989); **Jay Winter**, *The Experience of World War One* (Papermac, 1989).

Photo **p.7** © The Art Archive/National Army Museum London/National Army Museum

Every effort has been made to trace all copyright holders, but if any have been inadvertently overlooked the Publishers will be pleased to make the necessary arrangements at the first opportunity.

Although every effort has been made to ensure that website addresses are correct at time of going to press, Hodder Education cannot be held responsible for the content of any website mentioned in this book. It is sometimes possible to find a relocated web page by typing in the address of the home page for a website in the URL window of your browser.

Hachette UK's policy is to use papers that are natural, renewable and recyclable products and made from wood grown in sustainable forests. The logging and manufacturing processes are expected to conform to the environmental regulations of the country of origin.

Orders: please contact Bookpoint Ltd, 130 Milton Park, Abingdon, Oxon OX14 4SB. Telephone: +44 (0)1235 827720. Fax: +44 (0)1235 400454. Lines are open 9.00a.m.–5.00p.m., Monday to Saturday, with a 24-hour message answering service. Visit our website at www.hoddereducation.co.uk.

© Barbara Warnock 2012

First published in 2012 by
Hodder Education,
an Hachette UK company
338 Euston Road
London NW1 3BH

Impression number 10 9 8 7 6 5 4 3

Year 2016 2015 2014 2013

Typeset in Stempel Schneidler 11pt by DC Graphic Design Limited, Swanley Village, Kent.

Artwork by DC Graphic Design Limited

Printed and bound in India

A catalogue record for this title is available from the British Library

ISBN 978 1 444 15219 7

Contents

Introduction

About Unit 2

Unit 2 is worth 50 per cent of your AS level. It requires detailed knowledge of a period of British history and the ability to explore and analyse historical sources. Overall, 60 per cent of the marks available are awarded for source analysis (Assessment Objective 2), and 40 per cent for using own knowledge to form an explanation (Assessment Objective 1).

In the exam, you are required to answer one question with two parts. Part (a) is worth 20 marks and Part (b) is worth 40 marks. The exam lasts for one hour and twenty minutes, unless you have been awarded extra time. It is advisable to spend approximately one third of your time in the exam on Part (a) and the remaining two thirds on Part (b). There will be a choice of two Part (b) questions, of which you must answer one.

Part (a) tests your ability to:

- comprehend source material
- compare source material in detail, explaining how the sources agree and differ
- suggest reasons why the sources agree or differ based on their provenance
- reach an overall judgement.

Part (b) tests your ability to:

- select information that focuses on the question
- organise this information to provide an answer to the question
- integrate information from the sources and own knowledge
- weight evidence from sources and own knowledge to reach an overall judgement.

The Experience of Warfare in Britain: Crimea, Boer and the First World War, 1854–1929

The exam board specifies that students should study four general areas as part of this topic.

1. The impact of the Crimean War: significance of newspaper reporting; medical and nursing developments; pressure for army reforms.
2. The impact of the Second Boer War: propaganda; support for, and questioning of, Britain's imperial role; national efficiency campaigns; impact on social reform.
3. The experience of war on the Western Front: outline of Britain's involvement; medical and surgical developments; creation, recruitment and retention of a mass army; morale and discipline of troops; effectiveness of strategy and tactics.
4. The impact of the First World War on the home front; changing attitudes to the conflict; work and working practices; propaganda; organisation of the state for total war.

How to use this book

This book has been designed to help you to develop the knowledge and skills necessary to succeed in the exam. The book is divided into four sections – one for each general area of the course. Each section is made up of a series of topics organised into double page spreads. On the left-hand page, you will find a summary of the key content you need to learn. Words in bold in the key content are defined in the glossary. On the right-hand page, you will find exam-focused activities. Together, these two strands of the book will take you through the knowledge and skills essential for exam success.

▼ Key historical content

▼ Exam-focused activities

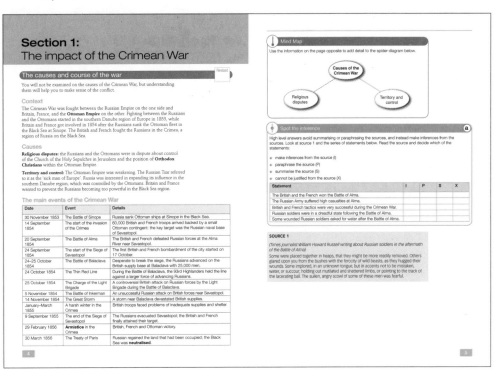

There are three levels of exam-focused activities:

- Band 1 activities are designed to develop the foundational skills needed to pass the exam. These have a blue heading and this symbol ⏺.
- Band 2 activities are designed to build on the skills developed in Band 1 activities and to help you to achieve a C grade. These have an orange heading and this symbol ⏺.
- Band 3 activities are designed to enable you to access the highest grades. These have a purple heading and this symbol ⏺.

Some of the activities have answers or suggested answers on pages 75–77 and have the following symbol to indicate this: ⓐ.

Others are intended for you to complete in pairs and assess by comparing answers and these don't have answers.

Each section ends with an exam-style question and model A-grade answer with examiner's commentary. This should give you guidance on what is required to achieve the top grades.

You can also keep track of your revision by ticking off each topic heading in the book, or by ticking the checklist on the contents page. Tick each box when you have:

- revised and understood a topic
- completed the activities.

Section 1:
The impact of the Crimean War

The causes and course of the war

You will not be examined on the causes of the Crimean War, but understanding them will help you to make sense of the conflict.

Context

The Crimean War was fought between the Russian Empire on the one side and Britain, France, and the **Ottoman Empire** on the other. Fighting between the Russians and the Ottomans started in the southern Danube region of Europe in 1853, while Britain and France got involved in 1854 after the Russians sunk the Ottoman fleet in the Black Sea at Sinope. The British and French fought the Russians in the Crimea, a region of Russia on the Black Sea.

Causes

Religious disputes: the Russians and the Ottomans were in dispute about control of the Church of the Holy Sepulchre in Jerusalem and the position of **Orthodox Christians** within the Ottoman Empire.

Territory and control: The Ottoman Empire was weakening. The Russian Tsar referred to it as the 'sick man of Europe'. Russia was interested in expanding its influence in the southern Danube region, which was controlled by the Ottomans. Britain and France wanted to prevent the Russians becoming too powerful in the Black Sea region.

The main events of the Crimean War

Date	Event	Details
30 November 1853	The Battle of Sinope	Russia sank Ottoman ships at Sinope in the Black Sea.
14 September 1854	The start of the invasion of the Crimea	60,000 British and French troops arrived backed by a small Ottoman contingent: the key target was the Russian naval base of Sevastopol.
20 September 1854	The Battle of Alma	The British and French defeated Russian forces at the Alma River near Sevastopol.
24 September 1854	The start of the Siege of Sevastopol	The first British and French bombardment of the city started on 17 October.
24–25 October 1854	The Battle of Balaclava	Desperate to break the siege, the Russians advanced on the British supply base at Balaclava with 25,000 men.
24 October 1854	The Thin Red Line	During the Battle of Balaclava, the 93rd Highlanders held the line against a larger force of advancing Russians.
25 October 1854	The Charge of the Light Brigade	A controversial British attack on Russian forces by the Light Brigade during the Battle of Balaclava.
5 November 1854	The Battle of Inkerman	An unsuccessful Russian attack on British forces near Sevastopol.
14 November 1854	The Great Storm	A storm near Balaclava devastated British supplies.
January–March 1855	A harsh winter in the Crimea	British troops faced problems of inadequate supplies and shelter.
9 September 1855	The end of the Siege of Sevastopol	The Russians evacuated Sevastopol; the British and French finally attained their target.
29 February 1856	**Armistice** in the Crimea	British, French and Ottoman victory.
30 March 1856	The Treaty of Paris	Russian regained the land that had been occupied; the Black Sea was **neutralised**.

Mind Map

Use the information on the page opposite to add detail to the spider-diagram below.

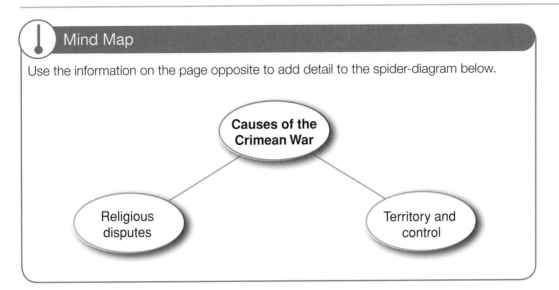

Spot the inference

High level answers avoid summarising or paraphrasing the sources, and instead make inferences from the sources. Look at source 1 and the series of statements below. Read the source and decide which of the statements:

- make inferences from the source (I)
- paraphrase the source (P)
- summarise the source (S)
- cannot be justified from the source (X)

Statement	I	P	S	X
The British and the French won the Battle of Alma.				
The Russian Army suffered high casualties at Alma.				
British and French tactics were very successful during the Crimean War.				
Russian soldiers were in a dreadful state following the Battle of Alma.				
Some wounded Russian soldiers asked for water after the Battle of Alma.				

SOURCE 1

(Times journalist William Howard Russell writing about Russian soldiers in the aftermath of the Battle of Alma)

Some were placed together in heaps, that they might be more readily removed. Others glared upon you from the bushes with the ferocity of wild beasts, as they hugged their wounds. Some implored, in an unknown tongue, but in accents not to be mistaken, water, or succour; holding out mutilated and shattered limbs, or pointing to the track of the lacerating ball. The sullen, angry scowl of some of these men was fearful.

The impact of war reporting – Russell and Fenton

The Crimean War was the first war in which newspapers deployed war reporters as eyewitnesses on the ground. War reporting had an enormous impact in Britain: new technology such as the **telegraph** meant that reports could reach Britain rapidly.

William Howard Russell and *The Times*

The Times was a very influential newspaper and had the largest circulation in Europe: during the war its circulation rose from 42,500 to 58,500. William Howard Russell, a reporter for the newspaper, was sent to the Crimea. His reports showed sympathy for the situation of ordinary soldiers, and he frequently attacked what he saw as incompetence by the army hierarchy and criticised army medical facilities and the poor living conditions of British soldiers. Following Russell's reports on problems with medical supplies in the Crimea, *The Times* established a 'Crimea Fund' in October 1854 to raise money to send supplies to the Crimea. Over £7,000 was raised.

Russell's reports provide valuable information about the conduct of the Crimean War. Not all of his reports are entirely reliable, however:

- After 25 November 1854, Russell was part of a deliberate campaign ordered by *The Times'* editor, John Delane, to undermine and attack Lord Raglan, Commander-in-Chief of the British Army.
- Russell did not witness all of the events he described in the Crimea in the winter of 1854–55 as he spent the winter in Constantinople and relied upon unnamed informants.

The impact of the press – political crisis: December 1854–January 1855

Following an editorial in *The Times* accusing the leadership of the British Army of incompetence and **nepotism**, a political crisis was triggered. The House of Commons voted by a two-thirds majority to establish a committee to investigate the British Army and the work of the government departments in charge of the war effort: as a consequence, the Prime Minister, Lord Aberdeen, resigned and was replaced by Lord Palmerston.

Roger Fenton and early photography

Fenton's photographs depict military camps, ordinary soldiers and their lives and the aftermath of battles: his images are notable for their unpretentious and un-heroic depiction of soldiers. From October 1855 his photographs were exhibited in London and then around the country.

Fenton's images have certain limitations as evidence because he was instructed to take no photographs of dead bodies. Also, many of his images were staged and he was not able to take pictures of moving people or objects.

The impact of the reporters

- War reporters and war photographers engaged the British public in the conflict to an unprecedented extent: the public were particularly concerned about the conditions experienced by ordinary soldiers.
- Russell's reports and *The Times'* campaign created pressure to reform the officer class and organisation of the army: after the Crimean War, reforms in these areas were made (see page 14).
- *The Times'* campaign also created a political crisis (see box above) which demonstrated the power of the press and public opinion.

Support or challenge?

Below is a sample part (b) exam-style question which asks how far you agree with a specific statement. Below this are two sources which give information relevant to the question. Identify whether the sources support, mainly support, mainly challenge or challenge the statement in the question and then give reasons for your answer. Consider the significance of the **provenance** (that is, who produced the source, when and for what purpose) of the sources. Hint: look at the date of each source.

Do you agree with the view that the British Army was well supplied during the Crimean War?

Explain your answer using sources 1 and 2 and your own knowledge.

SOURCE 1

(A photograph of British soldiers in fur coats taken by Roger Fenton in March 1855. By the time the photograph was taken winter in the Crimea was over)

This source **supports/mainly supports/mainly challenges/challenges** the view that the British Army was well supplied during the Crimean War because

_____

_____

SOURCE 2

(Part of a dispatch from William Howard Russell printed in The Times *on 25 November 1854)*

It is now pouring with rain – the skies are as black as ink – the wind is howling over the staggering tents – the trenches are turned into dykes – in the tents the water is sometimes a foot deep – our men have not either warm or waterproof clothing – they are out for twelve hours at a time in the trenches – they are plunged into the inevitable miseries of a winter campaign – and not a soul seems to care for their comfort or even their lives.

This source **supports/mainly supports/mainly challenges/challenges** the view that the British Army was well supplied during the Crimean War because

_____

_____

Depictions and remembrances of the war

The Crimean War has been remembered by the British as a story of brave, heroic soldiers badly led by blundering **aristocratic** officers. Certain events became very famous: the Thin Red Line and the Charge of the Light Brigade were depicted in a great many paintings, for example. You need to know about these key events and how they have been remembered and in particular about the controversy surrounding the events of the Charge of the Light Brigade. You should also make sure that you have studied Tennyson's poem on the Charge (see Source 1 opposite).

The Thin Red Line

Early on in the Battle of Balaclava (see page 4), Russian soldiers advanced on the British line. Organised in an unusual formation of two rows, the 93rd Highlanders stopped the Russians by firing volleys of **musket** shots. Watching from the hills above, William Howard Russell memorably depicted the soldiers as a 'thin red streak'. The soldiers of the Thin Red Line have been remembered as a symbol of the determination and heroism of the British soldier.

Commanders of the British Army in the Crimea

Lord Raglan: Commander-in-Chief of the British Army during the Crimean War. He died in the Crimea in June 1855.

The Earl of Lucan (Lord Lucan): Commander of the **Cavalry** Division which included the Heavy Brigade and the Light Brigade.

The Earl of Cardigan (Lord Cardigan): Commander of the Light Brigade.

The Charge of the Light Brigade

The Charge of the Light Brigade remains an infamous and controversial event in British military history. During the Battle of Balaclava, Lord Raglan issued a hurried and poorly explained order to Lord Lucan to charge at the Russians' guns. Lord Raglan intended Lucan to focus upon retaking British guns that the Russians had taken on Causeway Heights (a hill nearby). His orders were vague, however, and Captain Nolan, the officer in charge of delivering the message to Lord Lucan, was not able to clarify the order properly to Lucan. Lucan pushed ahead with the Charge, and mistakenly sent the Light Brigade down a valley where they were surrounded by Russian forces who attacked them from higher ground. The Charge of the Light Brigade has gone down in history as a horrendous military blunder accompanied by astonishing heroism of ordinary soldiers, although this depiction has been challenged by recent historians.

- Of the 661 who set off on the charge, 113 were killed, 134 were wounded and 45 were taken prisoner: the Russian casualty rate was similar. However, the Light Brigade were only saved from complete destruction by a French charge.

- Eyewitness accounts, such as Russell's, created the impression of a monumental error of army leadership and a tragic waste of life.

- Depictions such as Tennyson's poem reinforced this picture of blunder redeemed by the bravery and heroism of soldiers.

Highlighting integration (a)

Below are a sample exam-style part (a) question and two paragraphs written in answer to this question. Sources 1, 2 and 3 are the sources below. Read the question and the two extracts from answers, as well as the sources. Then, using a highlighter, highlight examples of integration – where sources are used together. You cannot reach Level 3 or Level 4 of the part (a) mark scheme (see page 78) without integration of the sources. Which paragraph reaches the higher level?

How far do the sources give a similar account of the Charge of the Light Brigade? Explain your answer using the evidence of sources 1, 2 and 3.

Paragraph 1

There are some differences between the sources. Source 2 describes the idea that the Charge was a 'glorious disaster' as a 'myth'. This is in direct contrast to source 1 which promotes this idea. In source 1 the soldiers are depicted as glorious in that they are shown as bravely fighting: 'their's but to do and die' and the Charge is also shown as a disaster as 'some one had blunder'd'. This is in contrast to source 2 which says that 'the Light Brigade had achieved its aim' indicating that the Charge was a success. Source 3 challenges this view in that it appears to suggest that the Charge did not work out well as it depicts 'chaos' as the soldiers advanced, and mentions the 'dead and dying men and horses of the first line'.

Paragraph 2

Source 1 shows the soldiers as very brave as they ride 'into the valley of death'. There has clearly been a mistake as Tennyson says 'some one had blunder'd'. This depiction is not supported by source 2 which says that 'the charge was in some ways a success'.

Explain the difference (a)

The following sources give different accounts of the Charge of the Light Brigade. List the ways in which the sources differ. Explain the differences between the sources using the provenance of the sources alone. The provenance appears at the top of the sources in brackets.

SOURCE 1

(From Alfred, Lord Tennyson's poem, The Charge of the Light Brigade, *written and published in 1854 in the immediate aftermath of the Charge)*

'Forward, the Light Brigade!'

Was there a man dismay'd?

Not tho' the soldier knew

   Some one had blunder'd:

Their's* not to make reply,

Their's not to reason why,

Their's but to do and die:

Into the valley of Death

   Rode the six hundred.

*Original spelling

SOURCE 2

(From Orlando Figes' recent book on the Crimean War, Crimea – The Last Crusade, *2011)*

But contrary to the myth of a 'glorious disaster', the charge was in some ways a success, despite the heavy casualties. The objective of a cavalry charge was to scatter the enemy's lines and to frighten him off the battlefield, and in this respect, as the Russians acknowledged, the Light Brigade had achieved its aim.

SOURCE 3

(From Clive Ponting's book The Crimean War: The Truth Behind the Myth, *2004)*

As the Light Brigade advanced up the valley, its pace steadily increased without any order to charge being given. There were heavy casualties from the start and, as the lines closed up, there was chaos as units became mixed together. The second and third lines were also disrupted as they rode over the dead and dying men and horses of the first line, which took the brunt of the fire from the twelve brass cannons at the end of the valley.

Medical and nursing provision during the Crimean War

You should know about the medical provision during the war and the work of Nightingale, Seacole and the Sanitary Commission.

Medical provision during the Crimean War

The major British hospitals were based at Scutari, near Constantinople in Turkey. Approximately 6,000 men could be treated there. Medical provision was inadequate with only four medical assistants for every 100 soldiers: provision of medical supplies was inefficient and hospitals were insanitary and lacked washing facilities. Consequently, disease was a very significant problem: of 18,058 British deaths, 1,761 were directly killed by enemy action and some died from their wounds but a great many perished because of disease. Poor sanitation and poor hygiene led to problems with **typhus**, **typhoid**, **dysentery** and **cholera**. Additionally, **anaesthesia** was only infrequently used and there was no treatment available for **septicaemia**.

The role of Florence Nightingale

Florence Nightingale, a British nurse, arrived at Scutari in November 1854 with 38 nurses. She collected information to analyse mortality rates and introduced improvements to the water supply, organisation, cleanliness and food at the Scutari hospitals. Using money from *The Times* Crimea fund, Nightingale bought supplies for the Scutari hospital: she acted independently of military authorities and purchased these herself. In the nineteenth century, Nightingale was turned into an **iconic** ideal of Victorian Christian womanhood in Britain and idealised as the angelic 'Lady with the Lamp', a **ministering angel** who visited and comforted patients at night. In the twentieth century some questioned her reputation and she has been criticised for her treatment of her nurses and for not doing more to improve sanitation in Scutari.

The role of the Sanitary Commission

As mortality rates in the British Army remained high (52 per cent of those admitted in Scutari in February 1855 died), Lord Padmore ordered a Sanitary Commission to inspect and try to improve the hospitals at Scutari. The Sanitary Commission arrived in March 1855 and identified continuing problems with ventilation and sanitation. The Commissioners recognised what Nightingale had not, that the entire sanitation system at the Barracks Hospital at Scutari was inadequate and they ordered structural works to rectify this. Mortality rates started to drop after March 1855 and were as low as 5.2 per cent by May 1855. The Sanitary Commission also worked to improve sanitary conditions at the British base at Balaclava.

The role of Mary Seacole

Mary Seacole, a nurse of Jamaican origin, travelled to the Crimea independently after British officials rejected her offer of assistance. Her company Seacole and Day established the British Hotel near Balaclava to supply provisions to the soldiers on the frontline. The British Hotel was also a place where soldiers could obtain respite and shelter. Seacole had some medical knowledge and nursed soldiers on the battlefield. She wrote about her experiences in her autobiography, *The Wonderful Adventures of Mrs Seacole in Many Lands* (1857). Seacole was popular and famous in Britain in her day, but her reputation was eclipsed for many years by that of Nightingale.

Use the information on the page opposite to add detail to the mind map below.

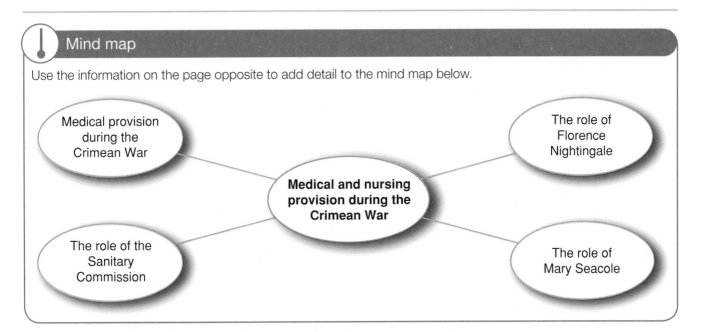

The following sources relate to the work of Mary Seacole and Florence Nightingale during the Crimean War. Read the information about medical and nursing provision during the war and write a part (b) exam-style question such as that on page 18 using the sources.

Use sources 1 and 2 and your own knowledge.

Do you agree with the view that

_____

_____

Explain your answer, using sources 1 and 2 and your own knowledge.

SOURCE 1

(An extract from Mary Seacole's autobiography, The Wonderful Adventures of Mrs Seacole in Many Lands, *first published in 1857)*

That the officers were glad of me as a doctress and nurse may be easily understood. When a poor fellow lay sickening in his cheerless hut and was sent down to me, he knew very well that I should not answer his needs empty-handed. Although I did not hesitate to charge him with the value of the necessaries I took him, still he was thankful enough to be able to purchase them.

SOURCE 2

(A recent account of the work of Florence Nightingale by historian John A Shepherd, published in 1991)

Miss Nightingale toiled without rest at the formidable tasks she had set herself. With all her administrative duties she continued to find time to visit regularly all the wards of the Barrack and the General Hospital. Frequently she herself undertook the nursing of those most seriously ill, or sat for hours at the bedsides of the dying. Countless letters were written to relatives at home, particularly to comfort the bereaved. She continued to fight for improvements in the conditions which prevailed, stirring the authorities into action, cajoling the senior medical officers, and constantly bombarding Herbert* and others in high position with her reports, suggestions and criticisms.

*A member of the British government

Disorganisation and inefficiency in the British Army

The Crimean War highlighted various problems with the organisation and leadership of the British Army.

Problems with supply and transportation

- Medical supplies at Scutari were inadequate. Basic items like bandages were lacking, as were more modern innovations like anaesthesia.
- In the Crimea, there was a shortage of wagons to transport the wounded to hospital and it took until early 1855 to get four hospital ships up and running.
- British soldiers were inadequately housed: they camped in tents during the Great Storm of 14 November 1854 and during the cold winter of January–March 1855 and lacked sufficient supplies of warm clothing.
- During the Great Storm, the ships the *Resolute* and the *Prince* sank carrying ammunition, winter clothing and hay for horses.
- Supplies that did reach the Crimea were often not effectively distributed and by the time they came to be transported were sometimes no longer useable: on one particular occasion horses starved whilst supplies of hay waited in Balaclava.

Problems with organisation

Problems of supply were partly down to overlapping structures in the British Army and a lack of co-ordination and clear lines of accountability. There were eleven different departments of the army and the government responsible for aspects of the army's supply and welfare. These included the Secretary of State for War and the Colonies; the Secretary-at-War; the Commander-in-Chief and the Quarter-Master General.

Problems with leadership

The leadership of the British Army was dominated by the aristocratic elite of British society. Officers often obtained their job through **purchase of commission** rather than through promotion on merit. This system came under attack as the failure to equip the army properly during the winter of 1854–55 and the perceived disaster of the Charge of the Light Brigade were attributed to poor army leadership. The top of the British Army was also seen as nepotistic: five of Lord Raglan's **aides de camp** were his nephews, for example.

Army leadership and reputations

The reputations of some senior members of the British Army were ruined by an impression of an inefficient and incompetently led campaign.

- **Lord Cardigan** was initially perceived as a hero after the Charge of the Light Brigade after he charged out ahead of his troops. He was later accused of deserting the Brigade at a crucial moment of the battle, however, and of incompetence in relation to his failure to distribute provisions in Balaclava Harbour. Cardigan later unsuccessfully sued an author who suggested that he had performed badly during the Charge.
- **Lord Lucan** received most of the blame for the Charge, accused of implementing an order he knew to be senseless and of failing to seek proper clarification of it.
- **Lord Raglan** died in the Crimea in June 1855 and was held responsible for many of the problems of leadership and organisation during the Crimean campaign.

Doing reliability well

Below are a series of definitions listing common reasons why sources are reliable or unreliable and also two sources. Under each source, explain why the source is either reliable or unreliable for the purpose stated, justifying your answer by referring to the following definitions:

- **Vested interest:** the source is written so that the writer can protect an aspect of their power, status, or position, such as their social class.
- **Expertise:** the source is written upon a subject which the author (for example a historian) is an expert.
- **First-hand account:** the account reflects a real event or experience. However, one account tends to provide only a narrow or partial view.
- **Political bias:** a source reflects someone's political views and therefore gives a one-sided view.
- **Propaganda:** these sources cannot always be relied upon as they are designed to promote a policy or idea, such as patriotism during a war.
- **Reputation:** a source is written to protect a person's reputation or status and therefore may be misleading.

SOURCE 1

(From John Sweetman, War and Administration: the Significance of the Crimean War for the British Army, *published in 1984)*

An inescapable fact during the winter of 1854–5 was that, as men went hungry in the trenches before Sevastopol, ample supplies lay in jetties nearby at Balaclava. But there were no means to get them to the lines. Sir John Burgoyne alleged that nine-tenths of all supply difficulties in the Crimea resulted from lack of transport.

> *The source is reliable/unreliable as evidence of problems with organisation within the British army during the Crimean War because*
>
> _____
>
> _____

SOURCE 2

(From George Ryan's Our Heroes of the Crimea, *a mass-produced pamphlet for a British audience, published in 1855)*

It may be said without fear of contradiction, that the Earl of Cardigan is now the most popular soldier in England… all salute him as the lion of the British army; and a clasp to the Crimean medal will tell how he led heroes to fight on that bloody field, which gives to the world an example of devoted valour unequalled in warfare.

> *The source is reliable/unreliable as evidence of the qualities of the leadership of the British Army during the Crimean War because*
>
> _____
>
> _____

Medical, army and civil service reform

The impact of the Crimean War on nursing

- Nightingale's work and her iconic status helped to establish nursing as a respectable profession for women.
- Nightingale's *Notes on Nursing* (published in 1860) was widely read and translated.
- Nightingale's name was used to raise funds to establish nursing training: £45,000 was raised by 1859.
- St Thomas' Hospital in London established a training school for ten nurses in 1860.
- Nightingale used her statistical work on mortality rates to illustrate the need for sanitary reform in all military hospitals; in 1857 a Royal Commission on the Health of the Army was set up.

Army reforms

One military development after the Crimean War was the establishment in 1856 of the Victoria Cross, the highest award for bravery in the British Army. In 1857, 111 Crimean War soldiers were awarded the Cross. The Victoria Cross embodied the new, more **meritocratic** approach in the British Army as soldiers of any rank could receive it.

In 1855, Sir John McNeill and Colonel Alexander Tulloch went to the Crimea on the instructions of the Minister of War to investigate the provision and distribution of supplies to the British Army. Their report exposed civilian and military mismanagement. Partly as a result of the McNeill-Tulloch report, Lord Cardwell, War Minister 1868–1871, introduced a series of army reforms.

The Cardwell Army Reforms 1870–1871

- Purchase of Commission was abolished: promotion in the British Army was now through merit.
- Conditions for ordinary soldiers were improved: the period of overseas service was reduced from twelve years to six; pay was increased and flogging was abolished in peacetime.
- The structure of army organisation was simplified and combined under the responsibility of one department, the War Office.
- The Commander in Chief of the army was made responsible to the Secretary of War and, through him, to Parliament.
- The country was divided into local regimental districts and each area had two battalions. One would stay at home to train, the other could be sent overseas.

These reforms were a serious attack on inefficiency and aristocratic privilege in the army. They did have some limitations however:

- **Entrenched** interests in the army resisted the reforms.
- No General Staff was established to engage in military planning.
- British **artillery** was not modernised.
- The 35,000 **reserve forces** were inadequate for fighting a European war.

Civil Service reform

The move to a more meritocratic system in Britain following the Crimean War also extended to the Civil Service where, during Gladstone's first administration, 1868–1874, all departments except for the Foreign Office adopted a system of recruiting by competitive examination.

Develop the detail (a)

Below is a sample part (b) exam-style question, one of the sources used to answer the question and a paragraph written in answer to this question. The paragraph contains only a limited amount of detail from the candidate's own knowledge. Annotate the paragraph to add in additional detail from your own knowledge.

> Do you agree with the view that the Crimean War resulted in significant reforms to the British Army? Explain your answer, using Source 1 and your own knowledge.

The Crimean War resulted in significant reforms to the British Army. As Source 1 says, the structure of Army organisation was simplified and therefore hopefully the problems of inefficiency that had occurred during the Crimean War would be resolved. Source 1 explains 'duplication of responsibility for military finance and supply had been largely erased'. This reform was significant because during the Crimean War there were too many different organisations involved in trying to supply and fund the army. There were also significant reforms to the British Army during the Crimean War in the area of the purchase of commission.

SOURCE 1

(From John Sweetman, War and Administration: the Significance of the Crimean War for the British Army, *published in 1984)*

The structure of army administration which emerged from the Crimean War seemed much simpler than that of March 1854. Duplication of responsibility for military finance and supply had been largely erased, the Board of Ordnance and (effectively) the post of Secretary at War discontinued. Curious anomalies, such as Treasury control of the Commissariat, had been resolved, the Ordnance Corps brought under the Horse Guards and a separate Secretary of State for War appointed.

 Recommended reading

Below is a list of suggested further reading on this topic.

- M Bostridge, *Florence Nightingale: The Woman and Her Legend* (London, 2008). See Section 5, pages 523–546, for a discussion of Nightingale's iconic status and reputation.

- Terry Brighton, *Hell Riders: The Truth about the Charge of the Light Brigade* (London, 2005). See particularly Section 2, pages 81–204.

- Clive Ponting, *The Crimean War: The Truth Behind the Myth* (London, 2004). See chapters 9 and 10, pages 160–214, for the impact of the Crimean winter of 1854–1855.

Exam focus

On pages 17–19 are sample answers to the exam-style questions on this page. Read the answers and the examiner comments around them.

(a) Study sources 1, 2 and 3.

How far do sources 2 and 3 support the view of source 1 about who was to blame for the events of the Charge of the Light Brigade? Explain your answer, using the evidence of sources 1, 2 and 3. **(20 marks)**

(b) Use sources 4, 5 and 6 and your own knowledge.

Do you agree with the view that the British army was poorly organised and led during the Crimean War? Explain your answer, using sources 4, 5 and 6 and your own knowledge. **(40 marks)**

SOURCE 1

(From Saul David's biography of Lord Cardigan, The Homicidal Earl: The Life of Lord Cardigan, *published in 1997)*

Lucan must bear the greatest burden of responsibility. By failing to insist on clarification from Nolan, he seems to have come to the inexplicable conclusion that Raglan expected him to save the naval guns by sending his division down the North Valley rather than along the Causeway Heights. He also failed to support them with horse artillery and to request the cooperation of the French cavalry.

SOURCE 2

(From Clive Ponting's book The Crimean War: The Truth Behind the Myth, *published in 2004)*

The primary responsibility for the catastrophic charge of the Light Brigade has to rest with Raglan. He was the man who issued unclear and ambiguous orders, with no idea of the difference between his viewpoint on the hills and that of the cavalry in the valley. However Raglan's orders were interpreted, they would have led to disaster either from an attack on the Causeway Heights or, as happened, from the charge up the valley.

SOURCE 3

(An exchange between Lord Raglan and Lord Lucan in the immediate aftermath of the Charge of the Light Brigade)

'You have lost the Light Brigade,' said Raglan bitterly when Lucan reported to him on the evening of the Charge. 'I at once denied [this],' recalled Lucan, 'as I had only carried out the orders conveyed to me, written and verbal, by Captain Nolan.'

SOURCE 4

(The Duke of Newcastle, Secretary of State for War and the Colonies in the British government, writing in 1854 on the British Army)

[The British army has been sent to war] in more admirable order, and with greater expedition than we had formerly any idea of, either in this or in any other country… I believe that such careful preparations never were made before.

SOURCE 5

(Written on 1 January 1855 by Frederick Dallas, a British soldier fighting in the Crimea)

What kills us out here is the utter want of system and arrangement in every department. Balaclava is strewed with wooden houses. The sailors make rafts of them; when nobody is looking they make firewood of them, but not a single Soldier has ever slept yet in anything but a tent. Hay, oats, biscuits, vegetables are rotting in the mud; yet the men until 3 or 4 days ago when they sent the Cavalry up with our rations, have been starving. It would be endless writing of all of the mistakes and absurdities committed.

SOURCE 6

(From Clive Ponting's book The Crimean War *published in 2004. Ponting is writing about the situation in November 1854)*

By the first week of November, as the weather worsened, the situation of the cavalry was becoming difficult. The horses had no shelter and there was no transport to take fodder up to the camp. By 12 November the horses were surviving on a handful of barley a day. Lord Cardigan, who was spending four to five days at a time on his yacht, refused to allow the Light Brigade to move to Balaclava where the horses could be fed. He also ordered that no horse was to be killed unless it had a broken leg or an incurable disease. The result was that the horses died slowly of starvation over several days, usually lying in the mud.

(a) Study sources 1, 2 and 3.

How far do sources 2 and 3 support the view of source 1 about who was to blame for the events of the Charge of the Light Brigade? Explain your answer, using the evidence of sources 1, 2 and 3. **(20 marks)**

The sources partially support the view of source 1 that Lord Lucan was responsible for the events at the Charge of the Light Brigade. Lord Raglan in source 3 agrees that it was Lucan, while source 2 blames Raglan, and Lucan denies it was his responsibility in source 3.

> This is a focused introduction that outlines the structure of the rest of the essay.

Source 3 backs up the evidence of source 1 that Lord Lucan was to blame for the disaster of the Charge of the Light Brigade. In source 1, Saul David says that 'Lucan must bear the greatest burden of responsibility'. He then describes a number of mistakes that Lucan made including failing to get the order clarified and not asking for help from the French. In source 3, Lord Raglan seems to agree that it's mainly Lucan's fault and that he made mistakes as he blames him saying 'you have lost the Light Brigade'. Lord Raglan's view cannot be entirely trusted, however, as he may want to blame someone else so that he doesn't take the responsibility.

> The similarities between the two sources are clearly drawn out and use is made of the provenance of one of the sources.

Source 2 does not support the evidence of source 1 about who was to blame for the events of the charge. Ponting thinks that it is mainly the fault of Lord Raglan saying 'he was the man who issued unclear and ambiguous orders.' According to source 2, 'however Raglan's orders were interpreted, they would have led to disaster.' This is in contrast to the argument in source 1 that suggests that if Lucan had got better clarification and more support the charge might have worked better. In addition, Lord Lucan in source 3 also disputes that he was to blame saying that he 'had only carried out the orders conveyed to me, written and verbal, by Captain Nolan.' This suggests that Lord Lucan blames Nolan's presentation of the orders, and also Lord Raglan in giving the orders. Here Lucan is in agreement with Ponting in source 2 that Raglan's orders were to blame. Lucan's view, however, is also unreliable as he too would not be likely to want to take the blame.

> There is clear focus here upon differences between the sources.

Overall, the sources partially support the view in source 1 that Lucan was to blame as source 3 agrees partially with this and source 2 does not. However, given that source 3 is not reliable as the Lords probably wanted to blame each other and ignore their own mistakes, the sources mainly do not support the argument of source 1.

20/20

This response has a strong focus upon the question and upon cross-referencing on points of agreement and disagreement between the sources. The response is logically structured and reaches a conclusion using the sources. The fact that source 3 may not be reliable is taken into account.

(b) Use sources 4, 5 and 6 and your own knowledge.

Do you agree with the view that the British army was poorly organised and led during the Crimean War? Explain your answer, using sources 4, 5 and 6 and your own knowledge. **(40 marks)**

The British Army was badly organised and led during the Crimean War, although there were some improvements by later on in the war. The sources back this up as they show the British army failing to distribute supplies properly and leaders making poor decisions.

The British Army organised its supplies to the Crimea ineffectively. In source 5, a soldier at the front line states the view that 'what kills us out here is the utter want of system and arrangement in every department' and that 'it would be endless writing of all of the mistakes and absurdities committed' suggesting that the British army in the Crimea was badly organised and made lots of mistakes. This may have been because the war effort was arranged in a chaotic way with lots of different government departments and sections of the army involved. The role of the Treasury and that of the army's Quarter-Master General overlapped for example. Source 5 is just the view of one soldier but it is backed up by other evidence like that of source 6 which talks about horses lacking food and shelter. In other areas there were also shortages, such as of medical supplies like chloroform. Supplies also often took a very long time to reach their destination. One consignment of hay took nine months to arrive. All this suggests that the British army was badly organised during the Crimean War.

Source 4 claims in contrast that the war effort was well-organised, stating that 'I believe that such careful preparations never were made before' but as this is the view of a British minister writing before the fighting had started, it can't be relied upon. However it should be said to support source 4 that part of the reason for shortages was that the Great Storm destroyed lots of supplies and that this event cannot be put down to the British army being badly organised.

Another way that the army was badly organised was that supplies were not distributed effectively. The soldier in source 5 talks of food rotting in the mud before it could be transported, whilst in source 6 horses do not receive their fodder because there was no transport. The author of source 4 would not have known about these problems as he was writing before the British started fighting. However, the transport situation did improve later on in the war after a train line was opened from Balaclava.

The candidate starts their argument with some evidence from the sources.

The candidate brings in their own knowledge to develop further a point from the source.

The British army was also badly led. Source 6 shows that it was not just a lack of transport that prevented horses from getting enough food but also that Lord Cardigan did not issue the correct order: he 'refused to allow the Light Brigade to move to Balaclava where the horses could be fed'. This turned out to be a huge mistake as the horses then starved. There was some complacency on the part of some of those leading the war effort as shown in source 4, as the government minister in charge believes wrongly that the army have been really well supplied and Cardigan was away on his yacht for much of the time according to source 6. Other examples that show that the British Army was badly led include the mistakes made at the Charge of the Light Brigade.

> A specific example of the candidate's own knowledge is deployed.

In conclusion, I agree that the British army was poorly organised and led during the Crimean War. Supplies were often inadequate and lots of mistakes were made. The sources back this up as sources 5 and 6 show that there were problems with insufficient supplies and that the supplies were not distributed properly, and sources 4 and 6 indicate poor leadership of the war effort as Lord Newcastle was not even aware that the army were under-supplied and Lord Cardigan allowed horses to starve.

> The strong focus upon the question is maintained.

39/40

This essay maintains an excellent focus on the question and the candidate gives a clear answer. Sources and own knowledge are integrated and a conclusion is reached using the sources. Specific examples of the candidate's own knowledge of the topic are included in places, although some points could have been expanded upon.

Reverse engineering

The best essays are based on careful plans. Read the essay and the examiner's comments and try to work out the general points of the plan used to write the essay. Once you have done this, note down the specific examples used to support each general point.

Section 2:
The impact of the Second Boer War

The causes and course of the war

The Second Boer War (1899–1902) was fought between the British Empire and the Boer Republic of South Africa. The British controlled parts of southern Africa while the Boers, who were the descendants of Dutch settlers to the region and usually farmers, controlled the Orange Free State and the Transvaal. You should understand the causes of the war in order to be able to place the conflict in context, and you should have some knowledge of the main phases and events of the war.

Causes of the war

Strategic: the British were interested in expanding their empire in southern Africa as this region was of key strategic importance to them as a route to India and other parts of the British Empire. They did not want to see the Boers join their territories to German possessions nearby.

Gold: Boer regions became more attractive to British miners and speculators such as Cecil Rhodes when gold was discovered there in 1886. The discovery of gold also worried the British as they felt that with this new wealth Boer areas would become too powerful.

The Uitlanders: the British were annoyed that the so-called **Uitlanders**, the mainly British foreigners living in Boer lands, were denied the vote in the Transvaal and the Orange Free State.

The main events of the war

The Boer War can be divided into three phases.

First phase (October 1899–January 1900): British defeats. On 12 October 1899, the Boers declared war on the British after the British refused to withdraw the troops they had gathered on the borders of Boer territory. The British suffered a series of humiliating defeats during **Black Week** and at **Spion Kop**, and were besieged at Ladysmith, Kimberley and Mafeking. The commander of British forces was General Buller.

Second phase (February 1900–June 1900): British victories. The British managed to break or **relieve** the sieges and capture key Boer settlements. In February 1900, Kimberley and Ladysmith were relieved, while Bloemfontein was captured in March, and Mafeking finally relieved in May. By June 1900, with Boer capitals Johannesburg and Pretoria taken, the British believed that they had won. The British commander during the second phase was Field Marshall Lord Roberts ('Bobs').

Third phase (late 1900 and throughout 1901): Guerrilla war. The Boers fought back with a determined **guerrilla campaign**. Boer commandos attacked British railways and supply lines. The British responded by destroying Boer farms, clearing Boer areas and establishing **concentration camps**. Eventually they gained the upper hand and in May 1902, the Peace of Vereeniging was signed: the Transvaal and the Orange Free State became part of the British Empire. The British Commander during the third phase was Field Marshall Horatio Kitchener.

Linking sources

Below are a sample part (a) exam-style question and the three sources referred to in the question. In one colour, draw links between the sources to show the ways in which they agree about the nature of the Battle of Spion Kop. In another colour, draw links between the sources to show ways in which they disagree.

How far do sources 2 and 3 support the depiction in source 1 of the results of the battle of Spion Kop? Explain your answer using the evidence of sources 1, 2 and 3.

SOURCE 1

(A report from the battle of Spion Kop by Winston Churchill)

Men were staggering alone, or supported by comrades, or crawling on hands and knees, or carried on the stretchers. Corpses lay here and there… the splinters and fragments of shell had torn and mutilated in the most ghastly manner. I passed about two hundred while I was climbing up. There was, moreover, a small but steady leakage of unwounded men of all corps. Some of these cursed and swore. Others were utterly exhausted and fell on the hillside in stupor.

SOURCE 2

(A British eyewitness account of the Battle of Spion Kop cited by Thomas Pakenham, The Boer War, 1979)

'We had no guns, and the enemy's Long Toms swept the Hill. Shells rained in among us. The most hideous sights were exhibited. Men blown to atoms, joints torn asunder. Headless bodies, trunks of bodies. Awful. Awful. You dared not lift your head above the Rock or you were shot dead at once. Everything was confusion, officers were killed or mixed up in other regiments, the men had no one to rally them and became demoralised….'

SOURCE 3

(From an account by Boer fighter Deneys Reitz)

We were hungry, thirsty and tired; around us were the dead men covered with swarms of flies attracted by the smell of blood. We did not know the cruel losses that the English were suffering, and we believed that they were easily holding their own, so discouragement spread as the shadows lengthened.

Recommended reading

- Denis Judd and Keith Surridge, *The Boer War* (2003). See particularly Section IV, pages 221–268 on the 'The Ambivalences of War' for some fascinating discussion of the role of the press and the attitudes of the pro-Boers.

- Thomas Pakenham, *The Boer War* (1979). See Part IV, Kitchener's Peace, for information on the situation in 1900–1901 during the guerrilla phase of the war, pages 461–571.

- The first two volumes of John Grigg's multi-volume biography about David Lloyd George contain much useful information about his opposition to the Boer War and role in the Liberal Reforms 1906–1911: see *The Young Lloyd George* and *The People's Champion*.

The impact of reporting and propaganda

There was enormous press and public interest in the Boer War, the first major conflict that the British had been involved in since the Crimean War. Newspapers now routinely deployed war correspondents and some, including Winston Churchill, achieved fame through their reporting and exploits.

The stance of the newspapers

Most newspapers were supportive of the war effort, and only the *Manchester Guardian* opposed the war throughout its duration. Anti-war newspapers found that their circulation declined, while pro-war newspapers enjoyed increased sales. It was for this reason that the *Daily Chronicle* hired a new editor and changed from being anti to pro-war. The *Daily Mail* (established in 1896) was by 1899 the best-selling daily newspaper in the country and was particularly enthusiastic about the war. The paper saw its circulation rise during the war, and benefited particularly when it dramatised events such as the **relief** of Mafeking. The *Morning Post* and *The Times* were pro-war but critical of government planning and organisation of the war effort.

The war correspondents

Most of the correspondents on the ground in South Africa were supportive of the war. However, many did not shrink from producing reports on British defeats, such as at Spion Kop, or from questioning army leadership after Black Week, when the British suffered a series of defeats.

- War correspondents were generally uncritical about the war effort and even sometimes put out false information to try to help the British – portraying the Boers as cruel and heartless, for example.
- Winston Churchill's reporting for the *Morning Post* increased his fame as he reported upon his exploits in being captured and then escaping from the Boers in December 1899. Churchill's stance was pro-war but he gave honest accounts of British defeats, the death and injuries of soldiers and the qualities of the Boers.
- Bennett Burleigh of the *Daily Telegraph* criticised the army after Black Week.
- HA Gwynne of Reuters news agency gave supportive accounts of the army's efforts in return for regular information from Kitchener.
- Emily Hobhouse reported on concentration camps in the *Manchester Guardian* (see page 26).

The army and the press

- The Boer War was the first to have an official British army censor.
- General Buller had a negative view of the press and did not co-operate with war correspondents. He consequently received a bad press after the events of Black Week.
- Field Marshall Roberts realised the value of the press in maintaining morale and in generating a positive public image. He tried to get press support by supplying war correspondents with information and allowing them to use army telegraph systems to relay despatches to London.
- Lord Kitchener felt that the press needed to be controlled. He introduced greater censorship during the guerrilla phase of the war in 1900–1901.

Below are a sample part (b) exam-style question and the three sources referred to in the question. In one colour draw links between the sources to show ways in which they agree about the role of the British press in creating public support for the Boer War. In another colour, draw links between the sources to show ways in which they disagree. Then around the edge of the sources write in your own relevant knowledge.

> Do you agree with the view that the British press created public support for the Boer War? Explain your answer, using sources 1, 2 and 3 and your own knowledge.

SOURCE 1

(George Stuart writing in his journal on 24 October 1899)

Behind the boy who brought his bundle of evening papers into Frank's shop, there followed thick, until the shop was crowded, men eager for War News. For so long they had been waiting about, with nothing to do, expectant of the stimulus, and desiring something truly stirring. They would like a bloody battle twice a day, so that breakfast and supper might have a relish, and ennui [boredom] be chased away!

SOURCE 2

(Historians Denis Judd and Keith Surridge writing about the British press during the Boer War)

Only one of the main dailies, the *Manchester Guardian*, stood out against the war. This principled stand cost the paper dear and by the war's end it had lost much of its readership. The *Manchester Guardian*'s only ally at the start among the dailies, the *Daily Chronicle*, soon became pro-war following a change of editor in order to stop the loss of readers. Only when the *Daily News* was brought by a Liberal consortium in 1901 did the *Manchester Guardian* gain a friend, but even they lost readers.

SOURCE 3

(Arthur Whitlock, remembering reactions to the relief of the sieges in 1900)

As these various places were relieved – Kimberley and so on – there was a great response of the people here. But I think most of all it was when we came to the final one of Mafeking, when there was a tremendous outcry of joy among the people there. There was shouting in the streets and such like and all the newspapers were full of that, particularly the *Daily Mail*. … It was a time of very great rejoicing. And we thought we'd turned the corner then.

Now try to write your own exam-style part (b) question using the sources.

Use sources 1, 2 and 3 and your own knowledge.

Do you agree with the view that

_____

_____

Explain your answer, using sources 1, 2 and 3 and your own knowledge.

Support for and opposition to the war

The majority of the British public, press and politicians were pro-war. However, a small group of radicals took a very public and often unpopular stance against the war. As the conflict dragged on into 1901 and reports emerged about concentration camps, support declined.

Supporters and opponents of the war

	Supporters of the war ('pro-war')	Opponents of the war ('pro-Boer')
Politicians	• The Conservative Party (who were in power) – Imperial Secretary and Conservative MP for Birmingham Joseph Chamberlain in particular. • The 'Limps' – Liberal Imperialists – the pro-Empire section of the Liberal Party.	• A section of the Liberal Party including young MP David Lloyd George who made a name for himself in opposing the war. • Leader of the Liberal Party, Henry Campbell-Bannerman, changed from pro- to anti-war after revelations about the concentration camps.
Newspapers	• The *Daily Mail* – who sponsored a Soldiers' Wives and Children fund. • The *Daily Telegraph*. • *The Times*. • The *Morning Post*. • The *Daily News* (until 1901).	• The *Manchester Guardian*. • The *Daily Chronicle* was initially anti-war. • The *Daily News* (after 1901).
The public	• The evidence of newspaper sales, the results of the 1900 'Khaki' election and the reaction of the public to British victories such as the reliefs of Ladysmith and Mafeking indicate that the majority of the public were pro-war. • The result of the 1900 'Khaki' election was a decisive victory for the pro-war Conservative Party. • Support for the Soldiers' Wives and Children Fund was strong – £70,000 was raised by the end of the war. • Support appears to have been particularly strong in Birmingham and London. • Some historians think that the middle class may have been more likely to be supportive of the war effort than the working class as the Empire brought the middle class greater benefits than the working class.	• Lloyd George's anti-war message was received most positively in Bristol. • **Irish nationalists** were anti-war as they viewed British **imperialism** negatively (all of Ireland was at this time part of the UK). • The results of the 1906 Liberal **landslide** election may indicate that the British public were less pro-war after the conflict had ended. The Liberal Party, containing a number of prominent anti-war figures, had a clear victory.

Reactions to the pro-Boers

Pro-Boers often received a lot of hostility, particularly during the early part of the war.

■ At a meeting in Birmingham, Lloyd George was attacked by a pro-war crowd and had to escape.

■ The MP for Liskeard, Leonard Courtney, received a very hostile reaction from his constituents when he made an anti-war speech.

Mind map

Use the information on the opposite page to add detail to the mind map below.

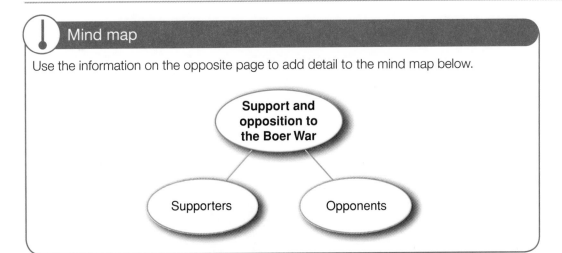

Write the question
a

The following sources relate to British public opinion about the Boer War. Read the information opposite on support and opposition to the war. Having done this, write a part (b) exam-style question using the sources.

Use sources 1, 2 and 3 and your own knowledge.

Do you agree with the view that

_____

_____

Explain your answer, using sources 1, 2 and 3 and your own knowledge.

SOURCE 1

(An extract from the diary of political activist Beatrice Webb in late 1899)

Liberals of all types are depressed and uncertain of themselves. The dismissal of Massingham from the editorship of the *Daily Chronicle* reflects the strong patriotic sentiment of its readers; any criticism of the war is hopelessly unpopular.

SOURCE 2

(From Denis Judd and Keith Surridge's book, The Boer War, *published in 2003. Leonard Courtney was MP for Liskeard in Cornwall. He was anti-war)*

An angry response was something pro-Boers in Britain would get used to over the next two years… pro-Boers who tried to speak at public meetings were often attacked, verbally and physically. Courtney's speech before his constituents was not only badly timed but let him in for howls of derision and the subsequent hate-mail.

SOURCE 3

(Minnie Way recalls what happened in Glasgow on the night that the news that the relief of Mafeking came through)

The relief of Mafeking – oh that was a happy night in Glasgow. My mother said the whole theatre that night just emptied and everybody ran to the public house for a drink. They were happy to know there would be some men come home from Mafeking.

Concentration camps and guerrilla warfare

You need to be aware of the nature of the British campaign during the guerrilla phase of the war including the use of concentration camps. You should have knowledge of the impact of Emily Hobhouse's reports.

The nature of the conflict and British tactics 1900–1902

The British declared that they had won the Boer War in 1900, but the Boers continued to mount a determined guerrilla campaign. Kitchener's response was to launch a **scorched earth policy** to try to weaken and demoralise Boer fighters: their farms were ransacked and burnt when they were absent. Eventually a system of **blockhouses** (mini-forts) established across Boer areas finally secured the territory for the British.

Concentration camps

During the guerrilla phase of the war, the British increasingly housed Boer women and black Africans from Boer areas in concentration camps. Poor organisation and supplies and inadequate sanitation and medical provision meant that disease and hunger were rife in the camps. Overcrowding also added to the problems: at their peak the camps contained 140,000 people. Children suffered in particular and cases of measles, typhoid, malaria, bronchitis and pneumonia were widespread. Death rates ran at the astonishingly high rate of 34 per cent in white camps. Black Africans were housed separately and received even less food and medical attention. It is likely that conditions here were worse, as one of Hobhouse's accounts seems to indicate, but no one troubled to investigate. An estimated 20,000 Boers and 12,000 black Africans had died in the camps by the end of the war.

Hobhouse's reports and their impact

- Emily Hobhouse visited South Africa and a concentration camp in Bloemfontein in January 1901. She wrote to her brother, a journalist on the *Manchester Guardian*, about the horrendous conditions that she encountered.
- Hobhouse's letters were first circulated as a report amongst MPs and later published in the *Manchester Guardian*.
- Many MPs and members of the public were outraged about camp conditions and Henry Campbell Bannerman, the Liberal leader who had previously been supportive of the war effort, made a famous speech condemning the British use of concentration camps and the scorched earth policy as '**methods of barbarism**'.

The Fawcett Commission

Millicent Fawcett, leading campaigner for women's **suffrage**, was asked by the government to go to South Africa to report upon conditions in the camps following Hobhouse's reports. Fawcett and her commission supported Hobhouse's findings and recommended that rations, hygiene and medical care in the camps be improved, and that the camps be administered by civilian, not military, authorities. Death rates fell to 6.9 per cent and eventually to 2 per cent.

Below are a sample part (a) exam-style question and a paragraph written in answer to this question. Read the paragraph and the mark scheme provided on page 78. Decide which level you would award the paragraph. Write the level below, along with a justification for your choice.

How far do sources 2 and 3 support the evidence of source 1 about British tactics in the Boer War? Explain your answer, using the evidence of sources 1, 2 and 3.

> Source 2 strongly supports the evidence of source 1 and source 3 mainly supports it. In source 2, Lloyd George refers to the British 'burning homesteads and turning women and children out of their homes.' This is similar to the depiction in source 3: 'the farms were burnt' and also in source 1 where the soldier says: 'we burnt hundreds of homes' and 'had to turn the women and children out in the wet'. All the sources agree that the British burnt Boer homes and put women and children out of their homes. Sources 1 and 2 give a very similar depiction of the British as brutal. The soldier in source 1 feels unhappy about what is going on saying 'it is a job that I can't stand and I hope we can get away from it soon,' while Lloyd George accused the British of fighting a 'war of extermination'. Despite the fact that one is a politician speaking in London and one is a soldier writing from the war both sources give a very similar story about British tactics and show them to have been brutal. Source 3 partially supports this as, by implication, Pakenham believes the British tactics to have been brutal: it is hard to see how women and children being 'concentrated in camps' can be viewed in any other way and the tactics are described as 'ruthless.'

Level: Reason for choosing this level:

_____

_____

SOURCE 1

(An account of a British assault on a Boer farm by Walker Henderson Thomson, an Australian fighting for the British during the Boer War.)

We arrived in Rustenburg after being away 3 months and were very much surprised to find that all the farmers that were living on their farms and had passes were out fighting again so we had to burn everything before us. We burnt hundreds of homes [in the] pouring rain and had to turn the women and children out in the wet with only a few clothes and very little food. It is a job that I can't stand and I hope we can get away from it soon. We came over to fight men, not women and children.

SOURCE 3

(From Thomas Pakenham, The Boer War, *published in 1991.)*

To deny the guerrillas food and intelligence, Lord Kitchener ordered the British army to sweep the veld [country area] clean. The farms were burnt, the stock looted and the women and children were concentrated in camps. ... I have found much new evidence that Kitchener's methods of warfare, like the ruthless methods adopted by many modern armies against guerrillas, were self-defeating.

SOURCE 2

(David Lloyd George, speaking to the House of Commons in July 1900)

A war of annexation against a proud people must be a war of extermination, and that is unfortunately what it seems we are now committing ourselves to – burning homesteads and turning women and children out of their homes.

The Boer War, imperialism and national efficiency

At the time of the Boer War, the British were almost united in their view that the Empire was necessary for British status and strength and was a positive force in the world. The Boer War was fought to enhance Britain's **imperial** status and control over southern Africa. You need to know about the way in which the war generated both more support for and criticism of Britain's imperial role.

The Boer War and support for the British Empire

- Patriotic and pro-Empire songs and poems were produced such as *Land of Hope and Glory* (words by AC Benson, 1902) and AC Swinburne's *Transvaal* (1899).
- Periodicals such as the *Boy's Own Paper* and the *Union Jack* were popular and encouraged people to feel pride in the Empire.
- Baden Powell established the Scouting movement in 1907 which promoted patriotic values.

The Boer War and criticisms of Britain's imperial role

Some opponents of the war broadened their critique to include a denunciation of imperialism altogether.

- Many opponents of the war criticised the motivations for it, claiming that it was fought to benefit rich businessmen such as Cecil Rhodes, who were in pursuit of gold mines. The Empire was portrayed as an enterprise designed to benefit rich men and not genuine national interest.
- JA Hobson, the *Manchester Guardian's* correspondent in South Africa, published a very influential book criticising the British Empire called *Imperialism – A Study* (1902). Hobson claimed that the British Empire served the interests of a narrow elite of arms manufacturers, aristocrats and international financiers whilst most people remained in poverty. His book was widely read by **left-wing** British writers and politicians and had some impact upon the wider British public during the 1906 election campaign.

The Boer War and the debate on national efficiency

The term national efficiency refers to the notion that Britain was losing its position as the world's leading power in the late nineteenth and early twentieth century. As Britain struggled to win the Boer War, some worried that Britain's national efficiency was declining. Problems with recruitment to the army during the war highlighted the poor health and physical condition of many in Britain: a third of volunteers were turned away by the army for these reasons. In Manchester, as many as three in five people were turned down. The worry was that poverty and the resulting poor physical condition of many British people would leave Britain unable to defend her Empire. Concerns regarding national efficiency were one of the motivations for the Liberal Reforms (see page 30).

Highlighting integration

Below are a sample part (a) exam-style question and two paragraphs written in answer to this question. Read the question and the two answers, as well as the sources. Then, using a highlighter, highlight examples of integration in the answers – where sources are used together. You cannot reach Level 3 or Level 4 of the part (a) mark scheme (see page 78) without integration of the sources. Which paragraph reaches the higher level?

How far do the sources support the view that the Boer War led people to question Britain's imperial role? Explain your answer, using the evidence of sources 1 and 2.

Paragraph 1

Both sources 1 and 2 support the idea that the Boer War led people to question Britain's imperial role. Judd and Surridge in source 2 say that the war 'caused the press to question notions of British imperialism.' Judd and Surridge are only talking about the press here rather than the British people in general, but source 1 similarly says that after the Boer war it was felt that 'national efficiency and Britain's imperialist future were alleged to be in jeopardy' as the war had revealed how many British volunteers were unfit to fight.

Paragraph 2

Source 1 shows that the Boer War may have caused people to question Britain's imperial role as it says that people were worried about the 'poor physical condition of working men in towns' during the war. This was because so many men (three in five in Manchester) were turned away from joining the British army because they were not fit. Source 2 agrees with this as it says the war caused 'the press to question notions of British imperialism.'

SOURCE 1

(From JFC Harrison, Late Victorian Britain, *published in 1990)*

National concern for health was awakened by army recruitment during the Boer War which showed the poor physical condition of working men in towns. At Manchester in 1899 three out of five volunteers were rejected as physically unfit. Seebohm Rowntree in his study of poverty notes that of 3600 recruits seeking enlistment at York, Leeds and Sheffield between 1897 and 1900, 26.5 per cent were rejected as unfit and a further 29 per cent were only accepted as 'specials' in the hope that a few months of army life would bring them up to standard – and this at a time when in order to obtain the required number of men, the army standards for health and physical development had been repeatedly lowered. These findings were confirmed by an interdepartmental Committee on Physical Deterioration which reported in 1904 and sparked off a good deal of talk about the 'decline of the race'… National efficiency and Britain's imperialist future were alleged to be in jeopardy.

SOURCE 2

(From Denis Judd and Keith Surridge, The Boer War, *published in 2003)*

The war, then, caused the press to question notions of British imperialism and revealed that even those newspapers most in harmony with the government would not tolerate what they perceived as a failure to uphold British interests properly.

Army reform and social reforms

The Boer War was the impetus for two highly important sets of reforms. The defeats that the British had suffered at the hands of the Boers prompted Lord Salisbury, the Conservative Prime Minister in 1902, to ask Lord Esher to make recommendations to improve the organisation of the army. Later Richard Burton Haldane, Secretary of State for War under the Liberal Government, made further crucial reforms. The national efficiency debate that had been partly triggered by the Boer War contributed to the Liberals' decision to pursue an ambitious programme of social reform which very significantly increased the role of the state in the health and welfare of its citizens.

Army reforms

The Esher Reforms

- Improvements to army organisation through better defined roles, such as that of the chief of the general staff, who had responsibility for planning and training.
- Improved training and professionalism through the introduction of new drill books and the establishment of the military training base at Salisbury Plain and officer training at Camberley.
- New and better weapons were introduced such as an improved Lee-Enfield Rifle.

The Haldane Reforms

- The British Expeditionary Force (BEF), a permanent, battle-ready fighting force, was introduced. The BEF made an important contribution during the First World War.
- The organisation of the Territorial Army (TA) was improved and it was strengthened. The TA also played an important role during the First World War.

The combined impact of these reforms made the British Army stronger, more effective and more efficient.

Social reforms

The Liberal Reforms of 1906–14

These were a range of measures designed to improve the health and well-being of the poorest in society. The reforms were introduced partly as a result of the Boer War. The Interdepartmental Committee on Physical Deterioration of 1904 highlighted how poverty and associated problems such as rickets weakened the physical condition of British people.

Among the measures were:

- The Free School Meals Act of 1906 – local authorities could provide meals for the poorest children in schools.
- The National Insurance Act 1911 made it compulsory for the poorest workers and workers in industries most prone to unemployment to participate in a government-backed scheme to provide insurance against sickness and unemployment.
- Measures were also taken to restrict exploitation of workers and provide medical checks for school children.

Develop the detail · (a)

Below is a sample part (b) exam-style question, the sources mentioned in the question and a paragraph written in answer to this question. The paragraph contains a limited amount of detail. Read the question and the sources and then annotate the paragraph to add additional detail to the answer.

Do you agree with the view that the Boer War led to significant reforms in Britain? Explain your answer using sources 1, 2 and 3 and your own knowledge.

I agree that the Boer War led to significant reforms in Britain. One area which was reformed was the British Army. As source 1 says, the Esher Report made recommendations to improve the army after the Boer War. The source shows how important these were as it says that without the Esher Report 'it is inconceivable that the mammoth British military efforts in two world wars could have been possible, let alone so generally successful'. The Haldane Reforms were also important changes to the army that happened after the Boer War, as source 2 indicates. This source, an extract from the Reforms themselves, shows that after the Boer War the army was reformed in an important way with the formation of a 'field force... completely organised as to be ready in all respects for mobilisation immediately on the outbreak of a great war'. This was to be important during the First World War. In addition, the Boer War led to significant reforms to social welfare. As source 3 says, free school meals and medical services for children were introduced.

SOURCE 1

(An extract from Britain and Her Army *by Correlli Barnett, published in 1970)*
The importance of the Esher Report and its consequences can hardly be exaggerated... without the Esher report, and its acceptance by the government of the day, it is inconceivable that the mammoth British military efforts in two world wars could have been possible, let alone so generally successful. The three essential recommendations of the Report were: an Army Council on the model of the Board of Admiralty; a general staff; and the division of the departmental responsibilities inside the War Office on defined and logical principles.

SOURCE 2

(An extract from a memorandum of RB Haldane on proposed military reform, published February 1907)
The National Army will, in future, consist of a Field Force and a Territorial or Home Force. The Field Force is to be completely organised as to be ready in all respects for mobilisation immediately on the outbreak of a great war. In that event the Territorial or Home Force would be mobilised also, but mobilised with a view to its undertaking in the first instance, systematic training for war.

SOURCE 3

(From British Public Policy 1776–1939 *by Sydney Checkland. The Poor Law was the system of state provision for the poor that existed before the Liberal Reforms)*
Already a new phase of welfare had begun. It was that of abstracting altogether from the poor law framework certain forms of care, and making them the responsibility of bodies outside the poor law. The provision of school meals and medical services (1906 and 1907) had given dietary and health functions to the schooling system under the Local Education Authorities.

Exam focus

On pages 33–35 are sample answers to the exam-style questions below. Read the answers and the examiner comments around them.

(a) Study sources 1, 2 and 3.

How far do sources 2 and 3 support the depiction of source 1 about conditions in the concentration camps during the Boer War? Explain your answer, using the evidence of sources 1, 2 and 3. **(20 marks)**

(b) Study sources 4, 5 and 6.

Do you agree that the British public supported the war effort during the Boer War? Explain your answer using sources 4, 5 and 6 and your own knowledge. **(40 marks)**

SOURCE 1

(From an account by Rina Viljoen, an inhabitant of one of the concentration camps)

There were a lot of diseases in the camp. People were often sick and many died, especially the children… and when the authorities learnt there was a sick child in your tent, they took that child to a hospital. And the Boer women strongly believed that within three days that child would be dead. You were also not allowed to visit that child in hospital. So if a child became ill you just hid him in the tent and kept him there.

SOURCE 2

(Dr Alec Kay, a doctor assisting the British, writing in 1901. By 'sexless busybodies', Kay is referring to Emily Hobhouse and Millicent Fawcett)

It is true that there has been sickness in the camps and that conditions have been primitive. But… there is always disorganisation and lack of careful planning where large numbers of people are moved. Improvements are taking place rapidly, and they would have taken place whether or not there was this agitation by sexless busybodies with nothing better to do than decry everything and everybody … I myself have worked at one of these camps when measles and influenza were raging. To children and adults, already debilitated by the results of war, anxiety, bad food and other hardships, any illness would be likely to become serious in the severe winter weather.

SOURCE 3

(From the report of the Fawcett Commission to the House of Commons in 1902. The camp at Heilbron had received a wave of people suffering from measles)

The death rate was very heavy, 10 dying on one night of the Commission's visit. Though some of the houses were comfortable, others were miserable sheds or stables… and yet a young girl, dangerously ill, lay in it. There is barely a language too strong to express our opinion of sending of a mass of disease to a healthy camp: but the cemetery at Heilbron tells the price paid in lives for the terrible mistake.

SOURCE 4

(Local newspaper the Handsworth Herald *describes the response in Birmingham to the relief of Mafeking)*

Staid citizens, whose severe respectability and decorum were usually beyond question or reproach, were to be seen parading the streets, shouting patriotic songs with the full forces of their lungs, dancing, jumping, screaming in a delirium of unrestrained joy.

SOURCE 5

(From Lloyd George *by Peter Rowland published in 1975. Here he is describing Lloyd George's experiences in Birmingham town hall in December 1901)*

By 8 o'clock the hall was jammed full with seven thousand people, the great majority of whom were waving Union Jacks, blowing trumpets or whistles, bellowing, chanting and singing and determined that the speakers should not be heard. Lloyd George rose to his feet, took off his overcoat and beamed at his audience. 'This', he began, 'is a rather lively meeting for a peace meeting.' He talked on despite the incredible din. Within five minutes of his rising to his feet, however, the audience made a huge surge towards the stage, at which point a squad of policemen concealed beneath it rushed out of their hiding place and an ugly struggle between truncheons on the one hand and hammers and knives on the other got underway.

SOURCE 6

(From Rosemary Rees and Geoff Stewart, The Experience of Warfare in Britain, *published in 2008)*

There seems little doubt that the war elicited widespread support and outbursts of popular enthusiasm. Much of the evidence for this comes from critics of the war like Beatrice Webb.

(a) Study sources 1, 2 and 3.

How far do sources 2 and 3 support the depiction of source 1 about conditions in the concentration camps during the Boer War? Explain your answer, using the evidence of sources 1, 2 and 3. **(20 marks)**

Sources 2 and 3 mainly support the evidence of source 1 about conditions in concentration camps. Sources 2 and 3 give a similar impression to source 1 of poor conditions in the camps, but source 2 also says that things are improving.

Source 1 suggests that there were poor conditions in the camps as disease was common. This is supported by sources 2 and 3. In source 2 Dr Kay acknowledges that 'it is true that there has been sickness in the camps'. Agreeing with this, source 3 mentions 'a mass of disease' at the camp at Heilbron.

In addition, sources 2 and 3 support the idea of bad living conditions in the camps. In source 1, Boer women don't trust British authorities so hide sick children; in source 2 the camps are shown as disorganised and primitive, although the doctor does say that this is to be expected in a war. Source 3 also describes poor conditions in some homes which were 'miserable'.

However, while source 3 mainly supports source 1, there are some differences. In source 2, Dr Kay thinks that conditions are improving, but there is no mention of this in source 1.

Overall, sources 2 and 3 mainly support source 1. All of the sources have their strengths and their weaknesses as evidence, however. All the sources are based upon actual experiences of the camps, and in the case of source 1, the lady lived through the conditions that she describes, while the doctor in source 2 worked in the camps and so would have seen what conditions were like. Source 3 is particularly reliable as an account of camp conditions, as it is taken from Fawcett's report, which was an objective outside investigation into camp conditions. However, the sources do have some limitations, as sources 1 and 2 are just one person's account, and the tone of source 2 suggests that the doctor is biased towards trying to down-play the problems, which may undermine the reliability of his view that conditions are improving, while source 3 only refers to one camp and so is a little limited. Taken together, however, the sources indicate that disease was very common and conditions bad at the camp.

> The introduction clearly answers the question.

> The sources are directly contrasted.

> The sources are treated as a group in order to answer the question. This is good technique.

16/20.

This is a focused response which compares and cross-references the sources and makes a judgement using the sources in combination. Good use is made of the provenance of the sources. The comparisons between sources could have been a little more detailed however.

(b) Study sources 4, 5 and 6.

Do you agree that the British public supported the war effort during the Boer War? Explain your answer using sources 4, 5 and 6 and your own knowledge. **(40 marks)**

I agree to a significant extent that the British public supported the war effort during the Boer War. The sources all give support for this view, although they also indicate that not everyone supported the war.

Overall, support for the Boer War was strong among the British public. Source 6 says 'there is little doubt that the war elicited widespread support and outbursts of popular enthusiasm'. This is supported by source 4 which depicts the ecstatic reaction of ordinary people in response to the relief of Mafeking: even 'staid citizens' were 'shouting patriotic songs with the full forces of their lungs, dancing, jumping, screaming in a delirium of unrestrained joy'. This indicates that people felt so strongly supportive of the war that even those who were 'staid' felt moved to join enthusiastically in the celebrations. This level of excitement about the war shows that people were very pro-war, at least in Birmingham, where the events depicted took place. Accounts of the public response to the reliefs of the sieges at Ladysmith, Kimberley and Mafeking show that reactions were very positive, which may indicate support for the war. In addition, other evidence also suggests that the British public were very pro-war. In source 5, the reaction of the public to anti-war figures such as Lloyd George indicates that people were pro-war. Source 5 reveals the very hostile reaction that Lloyd George received at a meeting in Birmingham at which he spoke out against the war. The fact that the circulation of strongly pro-war newspapers such as the Daily Mail increased during the war, whilst anti-war newspapers, like the Manchester Guardian, saw sales fall, also strongly suggests that the public were pro-war, as does the result of the 1900 Khaki election where the pro-war Conservative Party won a convincing victory.

The introduction gives a clear answer to the question.

Evidence from the sources is deployed to answer the question.

The candidate's own knowledge is used to extend the points made by the sources.

Support for the war was not universal however, and was stronger in some areas than others. Both sources 4 and 5 relate to Birmingham where support for the war was strong. In addition, source 4 may be exaggerated as the newspaper may want to sell more copies with dramatic reports. In other places, however, like Bristol for example, people may have been more anti-war, as Lloyd George received a favourable reception when speaking there. In addition there were a number of people who were anti-war, including Lloyd George himself and as is mentioned in source 6, Beatrice Webb. Also, support for the war seems to have reduced over time. By the 1906 election, the British public voted the Liberals into power on a landslide vote, after an election campaign in which questions had been raised about Britain's role in South Africa.

Overall, however, the British public were mainly very supportive of the war effort as source 6 states, the reactions of the people of Birmingham described in sources 4 and 5 suggest and as the evidence of newspaper sales and the 1900 election result indicate. However, not everyone supported the war, and support for the war may have reduced over time.

40/40

This is a well-focused and argued response which deploys the sources and own knowledge well to answer the question. Own knowledge is precise and specific.

Reverse engineering

The best essays are based on careful plans. Read the essay and the examiner's comments and try to work out the general points of the plan used to write the essay. Once you have done this, note down the specific examples used to support each general point.

Section 3:
The experience of war on the Western Front

The causes and course of the war

Revised

The First World War was a conflict of unprecedented scale. The great powers of Europe confronted one another in Western Europe, Eastern Europe and the Middle East. The war was fought between the Allies: Britain, France and Russia and the countries of their Empires, joined later by the United States and Italy, and the Central Powers: Germany, Austria–Hungary and the Ottoman Empire. You will not be examined on the causes of the First World War though knowledge of these will help to make sense of the conflict.

Causes

Long-term rivalry between the Great Powers of Europe

Tensions between the European powers intensified before the First World War, making conflict more likely. Conflict and competition emerged over the size of armed forces and an **arms race** developed between Britain and Germany over naval armaments and Germany, France and Russia over army size.

The alliance system

The formation of two groups of alliances added to tensions in Europe as France, Britain and Russia formed the Triple Entente and Germany, Austria–Hungary and Italy joined together in the Triple Alliance. Germany feared the possibility of fighting against Russia and France simultaneously and developed the **Schlieffen Plan**. The plan assumed that the Russians would take six weeks to be fully ready for war and therefore that in the event of a war, Germany had a chance to defeat France quickly before Russia was ready.

Problems in the Balkans

Conflicts and power struggles that took place in the **Balkans** were a source of instability in Europe before the First World War. The Ottomans had controlled this area but their grip had weakened and some countries like Serbia had asserted independence. In 1908, Austria–Hungary **annexed** Bosnia, a multi-ethnic state containing many Serbs.

Short-term trigger – The Murder of Franz Ferdinand, 28 June 1914

The murder of the heir to the Austro-Hungarian throne by Serb nationalists who wanted Bosnia to unite with Serbia caused a crisis as the Austrians blamed Serbia. Russia, concerned to prevent Austria–Hungary gaining more territory from Serbia, **mobilised** their army and the Austrians, backed by their ally Germany, invaded Serbia on 28 July.

The course of the war

The war drew in all of the European powers after Germany enacted the Schlieffen Plan. Germany invaded France through the flat and accessible terrain of Belgium on 1 August 1914. The British, keen to ensure that Germany did not get hold of French and Belgian ports and wishing to protect Belgian **neutrality**, declared war on Germany.

Phase one: 1914 – the race for the sea: After the British and French halted the German advance through Belgium and northern France in Autumn 1914, both sides raced to control the nearby North Sea coastline.

Phase two: 1915–1917 – static trench warfare: A front line was established running through Belgium and northern France. The two sides established trench systems. The war was primarily in a situation of **stalemate**.

Phase three: 1918 – a war of movement again: The German high command decided to launch one final push against the Allies on the Western Front in the Spring of 1918. Initial successes were short-lived however and by November, the Allies had defeated the German army on the Western Front.

Mind map

Use the information on the page opposite and add detail to the spider-diagram below.

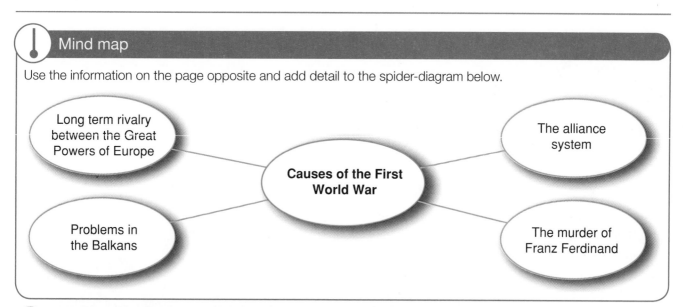

Long term rivalry between the Great Powers of Europe

The alliance system

Causes of the First World War

Problems in the Balkans

The murder of Franz Ferdinand

Doing reliability well
(a)

Below are a series of definitions listing common reasons why sources are reliable or unreliable and also a source. Under the source, explain why it is either reliable, fairly reliable, fairly unreliable or unreliable for the purpose stated, justifying your answer by referring to the following definitions:

- **Vested interest:** the source is written so that the writer can protect an aspect of their power, status, or position, such as their social class.

- **Expertise:** the source is written upon a subject which the author (for example a historian) is an expert.

- **First-hand account:** the account reflects a real event or experience. However, one account tends to provide only a narrow or partial view.

- **Political bias:** a source reflects someone's political views and therefore gives a one-sided view.

- **Propaganda:** these sources cannot always be relied upon as they are designed to promote a policy or idea, such as patriotism during a war.

- **Reputation:** a source is written to protect a person's reputation or status and therefore may be misleading.

SOURCE 1

(Vic Cole joined the British Army on 5 September 1914. This is his account of that time)

George Pulley (son of our local butcher) and I attended our first and last recruiting meeting. A leather-lunged gentleman was urging the crowd to throw up their jobs and fight. The way he spoke, it was just a matter of coming up, drawing a rifle and proceeding straightaway to France. The sergeant already had his eagle eye upon George and I and he was most pleased to greet us, possibly because of all the crowd we were the only ones to join up that night. When I got home, my poor aunt and Gran could scarcely believe their ears. Hardly waiting to close the door, I called out 'I've joined the army!' 'Oh dear! Oh dear!' said Gran. 'My poor boy.' Neither of them were at all demonstrative, but when I sat down, Gran put her old arm around me for a moment. My aunt shed a tear and then said, 'Well I suppose you'd like a cup of tea now.'

This source is reliable/fairly reliable/fairly unreliable/unreliable as evidence of the mood in Britain at the start of the First World War because

_____

_____

_____

_____

_____

_____

Trench warfare and the Western Front

Following the initial race to the sea, both sides reached a stalemate. A front line developed running from north-west Belgium down through France: the Western Front. This was the primary theatre of war for the British although there were also significant British and imperial forces in the Middle East. Trenches were built by both sides along the front line and over time these became more complex and better constructed.

Conditions in the trenches

There were a number of problems associated with trench warfare in terms of conditions for soldiers. These included the prevalence of rats, **trench foot**, and lice causing **trench fever**.

Trench conditions were dangerous: 31 per cent of those who served in the army were wounded compared with only 3 or 4 per cent of those in the navy or the air force.

The tactics of trench warfare

As the Germans were occupying Belgium and French territory, it was the British and the French who had to launch attacks to try to dislodge the Germans. This meant mounting attacks on the opposing force either through infantry advancing by going **over the top** through **no man's land** or by **bombarding** opposing forces with **shells** and **shrapnel**. Other tactics included the **creeping barrage** where advancing **infantry** would be protected by an arc of **artillery** fire landing in front of them. Another tactic, used by the British at Messines Ridge near Ypres in 1917, for example, was to dig underground towards German lines and detonate **mines** underneath them.

Tanks were an innovative technological development during the First World War. They enabled movement across difficult terrain. By the end of the war tanks were being used by the British as a method of breaking through enemy lines. A new and deadly form of warfare, **chemical warfare**, was also developed: poisonous mustard gas was deployed from 1915.

British weapons

Initially there were shortages of key items such as larger shells while the value of some of the weapons, like machine guns, had not been recognised by those more senior in the army. By 1916–1917 however, the British army was well-supplied with all of these items.

British weapons during the First World War	
Lee Enfield rifle	This very efficient rifle was issued to infantry soldiers.
Vickers machine gun	These machine guns, which could fire 450–550 rounds a minute and had a range of around 3,000 yards, were to prove very valuable in trench combat.
Lewis gun	This light machine gun was also highly effective in trench warfare and initially the Germans had no similar gun.
Stokes mortar	A small mortar which could fire 22 shells per minute.
Grenades and shells	There were initial shortages of grenades and bigger shells such as the howitzer but by 1916–1917 these were widely available.

Below is a sample part (b) exam-style question and the sources referred to in the question. Around the edge of the sources write your own relevant knowledge relating to the question.

Do you agree with the view that the British Army was well equipped on the Western Front during the First World War? Explain your answer using sources 1 and 2 and your own knowledge.

SOURCE 1

(From Hew Strachan's book, The First World War, *published in 2003)*

When Douglas Haig's attack at Aubers Ridge failed on 9 May 1915, Sir John French deflected blame from the army to the government by attributing the defeat to the lack of high-explosive shell for the British 18-pounder field gun, a misleading refrain which *The Times* picked up and which was in flat contradiction to statements which the prime minister, Asquith, had given in a speech to munitions workers in Newcastle.

SOURCE 2

(From George Coppard's memoirs of his time on the Western Front, With a Machine Gun to Cambrai, *published in 1969)*

The bitter cold formed ice on top of the sloppy mud, and it was almost impossible to achieve sufficient movement to circulate the blood properly. For men huddled in a few feet of trench or in the craters it must have been murder. … Fortunately, winter clothing had been issued, including sleeveless leather jerkins with fur attached, Balaclava caps with ear flaps and lined fingerless gloves. Many cases of trench foot developed.

Below is a partial answer to the exam style question above. Read the paragraph and identify parts of the paragraph that are not directly relevant to the question.

The British Army was fairly well-equipped during the First World War. Source 2 supports this as even though the soldier is describing horrible trench conditions he says that 'winter clothing had been issued'. Trenches were established from early on in the war. This clothing sounds good quality as it included leather fur jerkins and lined gloves. Later on in the war, the British also received steel hats which protected them from injury. British soldiers suffered hundreds of thousands of injuries during the First World War. The British Army were also well-equipped in that they increasingly had good weapons like grenades and the Vickers machine gun. Source 1 indicates that the British Army had sufficient weaponry as it reveals that, despite reports in The Times to the contrary (which are described in the source as 'misleading'), high explosive shells were in fact available, as Asquith had told munitions workers.

The Battle of the Somme, July–November 1916

The high levels of casualties experienced during the Battle of the Somme have led to it being remembered as a symbol of the suffering experienced by the soldiers sent 'over the top'.

The plan and the first day

In 1916 the Allies, Britain, France and Russia, decided to launch a co-ordinated attack on the Germans to try to break the stalemate. The British Army was now in excess of 2.5 million strong and General Haig, the British commander on the Western Front, was able to plan infantry attacks of enormous magnitude.

A massive German strike against the French at Verdun meant that the offensive at the Somme was primarily a British attack. German trenches were bombarded for a week in advance of the attack and the assumption was that much of the German trench system and the barbed wire guarding it would be destroyed.

On the first day of the battle, 1 July 1916, a huge British infantry attack was launched: soldiers were ordered to progress at walking pace to prevent panic and were protected by a creeping barrage. Events did not go entirely to plan, however, and the first day of the Battle of the Somme was the single worst day in British military history in terms of casualties. Overall the British and their allies suffered 57,000 casualties on the first day of the Battle of the Somme and 19,000 deaths. Many problems emerged for the British on the first day of the battle:

- Many of the explosives that had bombarded the German trenches were duds.
- German trenches were very deep and well-constructed and most were not destroyed: in fact German soldiers had been able to shelter in them from the bombardment.
- Much of the barbed wire remained intact.
- The creeping barrage had some success although it lacked precision.

The rest of the battle

The Battle of the Somme continued until November 1916. Although the Germans did eventually withdraw from the area, no major breakthrough was achieved at the Battle of the Somme and overall casualties were high at 1.2 million. According to historians Robin Prior and Trevor Wilson, British casualties were twice that of the Germans.

General Haig and the controversy over the Battle of the Somme

The length of the campaign at the Somme, the high level of casualties and the lack of a decisive result have contributed significantly to a widely held view of the First World War as one of cruel futility. General Haig's reputation, high in the immediate aftermath of the war, has been particularly damaged. He devised the battle plan and has been called the 'Butcher of the Somme' for sending wave after wave of soldiers to fight for so little apparent purpose. It should be remembered, however, that his tactics were standard for the time, and that the Somme also contributed to the **war of attrition** that was to ultimately grind the German army down.

Linking sources

Below are a sample part (a) question and the three sources referred to in the question. In one colour, draw links between the sources to show ways in which they agree about the situation for the British Army on the first day of the Battle of the Somme. In another colour, draw links between the sources to show ways in which they disagree.

How far do the sources suggest that the Battle of the Somme was a failure for the British? Explain your answer, using the evidence of sources 1, 2 and 3.

Add own knowledge

Below are a sample part (b) exam-style question and the three sources referred to in the question. Around the edge of the sources write in your own relevant knowledge. Now draw links to show the ways in which this agrees and disagrees with the sources.

Do you agree with the view that the Battle of the Somme was a failure for the British? Explain your answer using sources 1, 2 and 3 and your own knowledge.

SOURCE 1

(A British soldier describing the first day of the Battle of the Somme. He was writing at the time of the battle)

That those poor lads of the attacking parties had a real hell of a time is obvious from the lists of those who returned. From what I hear, the enemy were waiting for them with hundreds of machine-guns, bombs and rifles and it seems that the Germans met our attack with real courage. I can only record what I have been told by those who took part: that the Germans stood on the top of his trenches so that he could mow down our boys more readily, and Heaven knows, he did that only too well. Our men went down like grass beneath a scythe.

SOURCE 2

(Historian Jay Winter discusses the tactics used during battles such as the Somme in his book, The Experience of World War One, *published in 1989)*

After the failure of the Schlieffen Plan and the inconclusive nature of the battles on the Eastern Front there was a need for a drastic reappraisal of estimates of the probable duration of the war. Unfortunately it did not lead to a change in tactics, which still aimed at punching a hole in enemy lines, to engage in the decisive war of movement required by strategic thought. This approach made no sense in the first three years of the war, and cost hundreds of thousands of lives.

SOURCE 3

(Historian Gordon Corrigan discusses the first day of the Battle of the Somme in his book, Mud, Blood and Poppycock, *published in 2003)*

Planning was exact and the staff work preparatory to 1 July was superb. The troops were brought into position, the bombardment went as planned, even if the results were not as hoped, and it is difficult to see what else could have been done to minimise casualties. The reason that 1 July 1916 saw more British deaths than any other day in British military history is a combination of there never before or since having been a British offensive of such ferocity, against the main enemy in the main theatre of war, and the lack of experience of the troops and their leaders at battalion level.

The British Expeditionary Force (BEF) 1917–1918

The **BEF** had some success against the Germans in 1917 but no decisive breakthrough was achieved. By 1918, the BEF had honed its tactics and played a decisive role in the final defeat of the German Army.

The BEF by 1917

In 1914, the BEF numbered 80,000 men, but by October 1917 it totalled 3.9 million men. As the Germans concentrated on use of **unrestricted submarine warfare** to try to starve Britain into defeat, the British launched a major strike against the Germans near Ypres in **Belgian Flanders**.

Passchendaele/Third Ypres, June–December 1917

Passchendaele is also known as the Third Ypres because the front line near Ypres had already seen two previous battles. The main attack was launched in July 1917 and involved a skilful creeping barrage. The British had initial success, but poor weather and poor drainage rendered the battlefield a swamp. They advanced slowly and at great cost but had established dominance by October. Passchendaele was finally captured by December 1918: it had taken the British four months to advance seven miles. German casualties were 200,000 and British 250,000. Despite its reputation as a futile battle, and the fact the British lost the land they'd gained in March 1918, Passchendaele did contribute to exhausting the German Army.

The BEF in 1918

In Spring 1918 the Germans launched a huge offensive against the Allies. They met with initial success, and the British lost nearly all of the gains made at Passchendaele. However, Britain and her allies halted the German advance at Amiens in August, where Australian and Canadian troops took 18,000 German prisoners; the French and the Americans did the same at the Marne. The German Army were weak and overextended. The Allies launched a massive counter-attack, breaking the **Hindenburg Line** by September, and on 11 November 1918 the Germans surrendered.

The BEF, who took 188,700 prisoners and 2,840 guns from the Germans in 1918, experienced in 1918, 'by far the greatest military victory in British history,' according to historian Gary Sheffield. Why was the BEF such an effective fighting force in 1918?

- The BEF was skilled and experienced.
- Accuracy of guns and the creeping barrage had greatly improved since 1916.
- The British had sufficient artillery, a growing tank division and a large air force: British military production (organised by Churchill) outstripped German.
- Tanks were now more reliable and could be deployed to seize land quickly.
- The British could now advance using their creeping barrage, infantry and tanks at a rate of 100 yards every 3 minutes.

The improved BEF was not the only reason why the Allies won in 1918. Fighting was a joint effort between the Allied armies and imperial forces. In addition, the Germans were exhausted because of the strain of previous battles and the impact of the blockade on German ports. The arrival in 1918 of American soldiers also aided the counter-attack and the Americans helped the British and French with supplies and finance. Finally, the role of the Russians in wearing the Germans down from 1914–1917 was also important.

Spot the inference

High level answers avoid summarising or paraphrasing the sources, and instead make inferences from the sources. Below are a series of statements. Read the sources below and decide which of the statements:

- make inferences from the sources (I)
- paraphrase a source (P)
- summarise a source (S)
- cannot be justified by the sources (X)

Statement	I	P	S	X
In September 1918 the British Army advanced quickly.				
The Third Ypres was not worth the cost of fighting it for the British.				
British commanders were highly effective by 1917.				
General Ludendorff felt stressed in 1918.				
The British Army had some success in exhausting the Germans in 1917.				
British successes in 1918 were entirely down to the weakness of the Germans.				

SOURCE 1

(Commander of German forces, General Von Ludendorff, writing in his My War Memories, *published in 1919, about British attacks in 1917)*

The fighting on the Western Front became more severe and costly than any the German Army had yet experienced. I myself was being put to a terrible strain. The state of affairs in the west appeared to prevent the execution of our plans elsewhere. Our wastage had been so high as to cause grave misgivings and had exceeded all expectations.

SOURCE 2

(Historian Trevor Wilson from his book, The Myriad Faces of War, *published in 1989)*

Yet it remains a fact that, viewed absolutely, the blood cost of Third Ypres to the Germans was heavy. Plainly, it contributed substantially to the long-term debilitation of German fighting strength. Assuming the Allies did not run dry first, Germany could not go on indefinitely sustaining this erosion of its human resources… nevertheless… it was part of the culpable folly of Third Ypres that it caused the British Army to pay a greater share of the blood cost of ultimate victory than either the military circumstances of the moment or the long-term resources of the British people could justify in any way.

SOURCE 3

(From JL Jack, Trench Diary, *published in 1964. General Jack was serving on the Western Front in 1918)*

28 September 1918
The day's success had been astonishing; an advance of over five miles (more than in four months' bloody fighting last year). No doubt the hostile shelling had been less severe than formerly. And his infantry, behind ample defences, have not put up their wonted resistance. Nevertheless, allowing for every mercy (including our smoke screens), the good leading and drive of all our ranks from sunrise to sundown, through this bullet swept wilderness, has been admirable, hustling the enemy off his feet.

Write the question

The above sources relate to the campaigns fought by the British Army in 1917–1918. Read the guidance detailing what you need to know about the BEF 1917–1918 on page 42. Having done this, write an exam-style part (b) question using the sources.

Use sources 1, 2 and 3 and your own knowledge.

Do you agree with the view that

_____

_____

Explain your answer, using sources 1, 2 and 3 and your own knowledge.

Discipline and morale in the British Army

Discipline and morale appear to have been better maintained in the British army than in other forces as, unlike in the French, Russian and German armies, the British suffered from no major mutinies or rebellions.

Morale

A number of strategies helped maintain morale in the British forces:

Post: regular and efficient postal services were organised by the Royal Engineers Postal Section (REPS). In 1916, 11 million letters and 875,000 parcels were handled.

Food: the British Army managed to keep soldiers supplied with reasonable rations throughout the war. The French Army's ration contained more calories but was of poorer quality nutritionally and often consisted of just bread and wine.

Tobacco: tobacco was often issued to soldiers for free by the British Army.

Leave: many soldiers did not get home to Britain for considerable periods of time during the war. By 1918, however, all soldiers returned home on leave after six months.

Time away from the front line: most British soldiers were in the trenches for an average of ten days every month and only two of these days were at the front line. Troops received on average 70 days leave per year. The constant rotation of troops had some drawbacks, as soldiers were not always as familiar with their trench area as were the troops of other armies, but rotation helped to maintain morale.

Entertainment: behind the front line, entertainment such as concerts were arranged as were many sporting activities such as football and athletics.

Pay: pay for British soldiers was not high but those from the lowest-paid occupations, such as agricultural labourers, would have been better off than in peacetime. The lowest rate of pay was one shilling a day, but average wages were 50 per cent higher than this and soldiers did not have to pay for their food ration or clothing.

Discipline

Strictness of discipline varied across the British army between different units and divisions. During the war, 5,952 officers and 298,310 other ranks were **court martialled** and 89 per cent of these were convicted. The most common offence was being absent without leave.

Punishments

- **Execution:** use of execution by the British Army during the First World War has been controversial and, in 2006, the British government pardoned all soldiers executed for cowardice or desertion. Of the 5.7 million men who served in the British Army during the First World War, however, only 306 were executed for desertion of their posts or for cowardice. Having said this it should be pointed out that a number of those who were executed for desertion were young men possibly suffering from **shell shock** such as Private Harry Farr.

- **Field punishment number one:** field punishment number one was designed to humiliate miscreants. They were **fettered** and tied to a field gun for up to two hours per day.

- Other punishments that could be given by court martials included imprisonment, fines and demotion. Commanding Officers could impose extra duties or confine soldiers to barracks for minor offences.

! Highlighting integration

Below are a sample part (a) exam-style question and a paragraph written in answer to this question. Read the question and the answer, as well as the sources. Then, using a highlighter, highlight examples of integration – where the sources are used together. You cannot reach Level 3 or Level 4 on the part (a) mark scheme (see page 78) without integration of the sources. What level would you give the paragraph?

How far do the sources suggest that military justice in the British Army was oppressive and unfair? Explain your answer, using the evidence of sources 1, 2 and 3.

The sources partially support the idea that military justice was oppressive and unfair. In sources 2 and 3 a negative view is given of the use of the death penalty by the British Army. In source 3, the Colonel says that execution 'seemed like cold-blooded murder'. This is supported by source 2 where the soldier 'Duck' who has been executed is portrayed in a positive light implying that he should not have been executed. Both the sources also imply that military justice is unfair and oppressive by the impact that the executions seem to have on soldiers in the British Army. In source 3 everyone is 'thoroughly depressed at the thought of the fellow waiting in his barn for a cold dawn and death' whilst in source 2 the solder says 'we thought justice was a bit off the mark.' The implication in source 2, that military justice was unfair because judges made arbitrary decisions as guilty verdicts were handed out when 'the superior officer is not feeling too well at the trial', is refuted by source 1 however where Corrigan argues that trials were conducted fairly with the same rules of evidence as civilian trials.

SOURCE 1

(Gordon Corrigan writing in 2003 in his book, Mud, Blood and Poppycock*)*

This is not to say that military justice in 1914–1918 was oppressive or unfair. Sections of the Army Act were regularly read out to soldiers on parade: there was no excuse for not knowing the law, or for not being fully aware of the punishments that might be inflicted for contravening it. The rules of evidence in military law were exactly the same as those in civilian law, and the rights of the accused were laid down in detail in all the rules of procedure.

SOURCE 2

(A British soldier of the First World War commenting on army discipline. 'Duck' was his friend)

Duck sentenced to death, as good a man as we had, the biggest comic, only fond of drink. We did'nt [sic] know much about court-martials, or any martials, but if these were the kind of men that got sentenced to death, we thought justice was a bit off the mark. … We think quite a lot about this business. First, death sentences seem to be given if the superior officer is not feeling too well at the trial, and second, if the front line is to remain for two years, theres [sic] more than Duck has got the death sentence.

SOURCE 3

(Colonel Walter Norris Nicholson who served on the Western Front during the First World War expresses his views on the use of the death penalty by the British Army)

Once we had a deserter who was tried, condemned and shot. To make all arrangements, guard, firing part, burial part, chaplain and doctor, was quite horrible… it seemed like cold-blooded murder, and all were thoroughly depressed at the thought of the fellow waiting in his barn for a cold dawn and death. Our casualty list included many deaths; but they all had a sporting chance, which this fellow did not.

Medical and surgical developments

Medical provision

Medical provision was organised by the Royal Army Medical Corps. Provision was generally good with one hospital ship and one hospital train assigned to each division. Ambulances, field dressing stations and hospitals were quickly established. One problem was a shortage of doctors, however, and large numbers of volunteer doctors from the United States had to be deployed. By 1918, 23,000 nurses were employed by British forces, supplemented by 38,000 members of the Voluntary Aid Detachment (VAD) who undertook roles as nurses, ambulance drivers and cooks. In comparison with earlier conflicts, pain relief such as morphine was more available, while stomach disorders such as typhoid and dysentery were much less common. Inoculation against typhoid and improved hygiene reduced the incidence of the disease to only 2 per cent of that of the Boer War and for the first time, more soldiers died from battle wounds than from disease (740,000 to 84,000).

Infection

A major problem facing medical treatment during the First World War was that of infection. Lack of antibiotics meant that most wounds went septic. **Gangrene** frequently set in and was a big killer. Shrapnel, shell fragments and bullets often remained within the body and sometimes created septicaemia.

Injury

Trench warfare, shelling and gas all created significant problems with injury. British soldiers experienced:

- 41,000 amputations
- 272,000 additional injuries to the arms or legs
- 60,500 wounds to head or eyes
- 89,000 other serious wounds to the body.

Medical developments

In a number of areas of medicine the experiences of treating soldiers during the war led to innovations and new thinking:

- **Psychiatry and 'shell shock' or neurasthenia:** the war was the first conflict in which the psychological impact that fighting might have upon soldiers was seriously considered. Shell shock was recognised from 1915 and the Mental Health Bill of 1915 provided for the treatment of mental disorder resulting from war. Shell shock was initially thought to be a caused by a **physiological** reaction to exploding shells. It was gradually recognised that a cause of the condition was the **psychological** toll that war could take. By the end of the war there had been 80,000 cases of shell shock diagnosed.
- **Blood transfusions:** these were developed in field hospitals during the war although, as transfusions were an innovative treatment, most of those who suffered major **haemorrhages** died.
- **Skin grafts:** Harold Gillies developed the use of plastic surgery to treat soldiers with facial injuries through pioneering use of skin transplants. He was one of the first surgeons to consider the impact of his work on a patient's appearance.
- **Brain surgery:** improvements in treatment for brain injury enhanced survival rates during the First World War.
- **Prosthetics and orthopaedics:** artificial limbs were greatly improved as a response to the high numbers of injured soldiers with missing limbs.

Below is a sample part (a) exam-style question which asks how far you agree with a specific statement. Below this are two sources which give information relevant to the question. Identify whether the sources support, mainly support, mainly challenge or challenge the statement in the question and then give reasons for your answer. Consider the significance of the provenance (that is, who produced the source, when and for what purpose) of the sources.

How far do the sources suggest that the soldiers suffering from shell shock were well treated by British military authorities during the First World War? Explain your answer, using the evidence of source 1 and 2.

SOURCE 1

(From a report by Army psychiatrist Major-General Sir WP MacPherson and his team)

Any soldier above the rank of corporal seemed possessed of too much dignity to become hysterical.

> This source **supports/mainly supports/ mainly challenges/challenges** the view that soldiers suffering from shell shock were well treated by British military authorities during the First World War because
>
> _____
>
> _____

SOURCE 2

(George Coppard served on the Western Front. This is an extract from his memoir, With a Machine Gun to Cambrai, *published in 1969. The Hohenzollern Redoubt was a German fortification which the British attacked in 1915)*

Prolonged exposure to siege warfare conditions of the type which prevailed in the Hohenzollern Redoubt seriously affected the morale and nervous systems of men not physically capable of endurance. If any poor devil's nerves got the better of him, and he was found wandering behind the lines, a not infrequent occurrence, it was prima facie a cowardice or desertion case. There was no psychiatric defence available to help save him from a firing squad. The RAMC* knew little about mental distress brought on by the violence of war, or if they did little was done about it. It is my considered opinion that some men who met their end before a firing squad

> This source **supports/mainly supports/ mainly challenges/challenges** the view that soldiers suffering from shell shock were well treated by British military authorities during the First World War because
>
> _____
>
> _____

would have willingly fought the enemy in hand-to-hand combat, but they simply could not endure prolonged shell and mortar fire.

*Royal Army Medical Corps

 Recommended reading

- J Bourke, *Dismembering the Male – Men's bodies, Britain and the Great War* (1996). See particularly Chapter 1 'Mutilating' for some of the impact of the fighting in terms of injuries and Chapter 2 'Malingering' for discussion of the psychological impact of the war (pages 31–123).

- G Coppard *With a Machine Gun to Cambrai* (1969). A short and lively first-hand account of fighting on the Western Front.

- J Keegan *The First World War* (1998). A comprehensive and accessible account of the First World War. See Chapter 6 'Stalemate' pages 189–220 for an account of the Western Front.

- G Sheffield *Forgotten Victory* (2001). This is a **revisionist** account of the war. See Chapter 9, pages 221–263 for information about victory in 1918.

Exam focus

On pages 50–53 are sample answers to the exam-style questions below. Read the answers and the examiner comments around them.

(a) Study sources 1, 2 and 3.

How far do sources 1, 2 and 3 support the view that British tactics were effective during the First World War? Explain your answer, using the evidence of sources 1, 2 and 3. **(20 marks)**

(b) Use sources 4, 5 and 6 and your own knowledge.

Do you agree with the view that conditions were good for British soldiers on the Western Front during the First World War? Explain your answer, using sources 4, 5 and 6 and your own knowledge.

(40 marks)

SOURCE 1

(Basil Liddell Hart writing in 1916. Liddell Hart was a serving soldier at this point. He was later a writer and theorist on military matters)

Things of Which I am Proud. Being present at the introduction of the creeping barrage and knowing of its invention. This wonderful wall of bursting shells, which searches every inch of ground as it creeps forward over German lines, and yet is so marvellously accurate that our infantry can follow within fifty to one hundred yards of it, is the outstanding tactical innovation of the war… this creeping barrage proved so successful that shortly after the British Army as a whole adopted it … the French copied it from us.

SOURCE 2

(From a history textbook published in 1982. The Battle of Cambrai was fought November–December 1917)

The Battle of Cambrai … demonstrated that tanks, properly used, might break the deadlock of trench warfare. 381 massed British tanks made a great breach in the German line, but the lack of reserves prevented the success from being followed up. However, the lesson had been observed and Cambrai became the model for the successful attacks of 1918.

SOURCE 3

(From a book by historians Robin Prior and Trevor Wilson, The Somme, *published in 2006)*

In 1916, as every battle in 1915 had demonstrated, the only sure way of proceeding was to accumulate such weaponry and shells as could blast the enemy from one defensive line to another, along the way ensuring that the casualties of the attacking side were minimised and those on the defending side maximised. The aim of an 'attritional' general was not therefore to gain ground but to kill the enemy in such numbers that his powers of resistance would be gradually worn down. Haig did not have the deadlines, fixity of purpose, or the type of mind that could make the precise calculations of the munitions and guns required to achieve such results.

SOURCE 4

(The reminiscence of Charlie Miles, a private in the 10th Battalion, Royal Fusiliers, during Third Ypres)

As a runner, finding your way around in that sea of mud was the worst part. … The moment you set off you felt that dreadful suction. It was forever pulling you down, and you could hear the sound of your feet coming out in a kind of sucking 'plop' that seemed much louder at night when you were on your own. In a way, it was worse when the mud didn't suck you down; when it yielded under your feet you knew that it was a body you were treading on. It was terrifying. You'd tread on one on the stomach, perhaps, and it would grunt all the air out of its body. … The smell could make you vomit.

SOURCE 5

(From Gordon Corrigan, Mud, Blood and Poppycock, *published in 2003)*

The British Army took great pains to ensure that men were regularly rotated between front-line positions and billets to the rear. With a division having two of its brigades in the lines and one out, and with each brigade having two of its four battalions in the line, a battalion could expect, on average, to spend just ten days a month in the trenches. In practice this varied with the tactical situation: more men would be in the line when a German attack was imminent, or when the British planned to take the offensive.

SOURCE 6

(From John Nettleton, The Anger of Guns: An Infantry Officer on the Western Front, *published in 1979)*

A lot of hot air has been talked about the iniquity of [field punishment number one], but I cannot see that it was so terrible. You were not lashed to the wagon wheel; you were never kept there for longer than an hour at a time; you were loosed if it got too hot or too cold or if it rained, so there was little physical discomfort. Presumably, it was the moral effect that was supposed to be the deterrent.

(a) Study sources 1, 2 and 3.

How far do sources 2 and 3 support the view that British tactics were effective during the First World War? Explain your answer, using the evidence of sources 1, 2 and 3. **(20 marks)**

The sources support the idea that the British developed effective tactics to a certain extent, as sources 1 and 2 indicate. However, this was really only later on in the war and source 3 questions the effectiveness of tactics at the Battle of the Somme.

Sources 1 and 2 indicate that British tactics on the Western Front were effective during the First World War. Basil Liddell Hart in source 1 was obviously impressed by the creeping barrage that he had witnessed in 1916, and this suggests that this new tactic was effective at this time. Liddell Hart indicates this by saying that it is 'wonderful' and 'marvellous'. This is similar to the language of the 'successful' tactics mentioned in source 2. The sources also suggest that the tactics of the British were effective as they were copied and used again. In source 1, Hart says that 'this creeping barrage proved so successful that shortly after the British Army as a whole adopted it... the French copied it from us', suggesting that the French must have viewed it to be a good technique on the Western Front. Likewise, in source 2, it is seen that at Cambrai, the British had used successful tactics in relation to deployment of tanks as an offensive weapon and that this was something copied and used again by British forces in 1918, implying that these tactics contributed to winning the war.

However, the sources suggest that British tactics were not entirely successful. Liddell Hart was writing in 1916 before the Battle of the Somme where, although the creeping barrage might have had some successes, the British suffered huge casualties and did not score a decisive victory. Similarly, source 2 shows that at Cambrai, despite the tank tactics, the British did not achieve a victory.

A clear answer to the question is given immediately and the sources are used.

Sources are used in combination to answer the question.

This is supported by source 3 which indicates that, at least in 1916 at the Somme, British tactics were not very effective. Wilson and Prior implicitly criticise the high British casualties at the Somme and suggest that Haig, in charge at the Somme 'did not have the deadlines, fixity of purpose, or the type of mind that could make the precise calculations of the munitions and guns required'. This indicates that these authors think that tactics designed by Haig at the Somme were not effective and the tone here differs significantly from Hart's excitement in source 1 about the possibilities of the creeping barrage.

Overall, the sources indicate that British tactics were somewhat successful, at least by the end of the war when, as source 2 indicates, the British were able to deploy tanks very successfully. Source 1 would appear to suggest similarly that the tactic of creeping barrage was highly effective and precise. However, Hart's is just one person's account and there is insufficient information to judge whether the tactic was successful throughout the war. His reliability is undermined somewhat by the fact that source 3, by two historians who are presumably experts, reveals problems with tactics in 1916, when Hart was writing. As he was later a military expert, however, he was probably a good person to comment on tactics. Source 3 indicates that tactics were not effective in 1916, and source 2 that they were only partially effective in 1917, and so overall, the sources suggest that British tactics were not entirely effective until 1918.

The significance of the provenance of the sources is considered.

20/20

This response demonstrates a clear focus upon the question, with sources used in combination to reach judgements. Effective use is made of the provenance of the sources and precise details are deployed from the sources.

(b) Use sources 4, 5 and 6 and your own knowledge.

Do you agree with the view that British soldiers were looked after well and fairly treated on the Western Front during the First World War? Explain your answer, using sources 4, 5 and 6 and your own knowledge. **(40 marks)**

I do not agree that British soldiers were always looked after well and fairly treated, as trench and fighting conditions were often horrendous as source 4 suggests. However, British soldiers did at least get to spend considerable time away from the front line trenches, as source 5 shows.

Conditions for British soldiers on the Western Front were difficult as soldiers frequently experienced poor trench conditions as described by the private in source 4. Miles indicates some of the problems that soldiers faced in terms of the mud, which often contained concealed dead bodies which soldiers might step on: 'you knew that it was a body you were treading on. It was terrifying.' The fact that Miles describes this as 'terrifying' indicates that British soldiers were not well looked after. Additionally, spending so much time having to confront death and destruction was very difficult and some soldiers developed shell shock and broke down from the strain fighting the war. Further, conditions for soldiers were poor because of other problems associated with trenches, such as rats, lice and trench foot. It was unpleasant in the trenches and soldiers were sometimes made ill by it.

In addition, British soldiers were not always fairly treated, because of the harsh discipline that they faced. In source 6, the officer describes Field Punishment Number One, where someone might be tied to a gun as a punishment. The officer 'cannot see that it was so terrible' but does admit that it had a 'moral' effect, so presumably would be humiliating. Furthermore, some soldiers were shot for cowardice by the British Army, which would indicate oppressive discipline and therefore suggest that soldiers were not treated fairly.

However, there were some positives about the conditions for British soldiers that would suggest that in the context of a big war, they were reasonably well looked after. Source 5 indicates that the British Army made a big effort to ensure that soldiers spent some time away from the front line trenches: Corrigan writes that 'the British Army took great pains to ensure that men were regularly rotated between front-line positions and billets to the rear' where they would have been away from the fighting and the poor trench conditions. Corrigan says that soldiers only spent 10 days a month in the trenches on average. He does acknowledge, however, that this varied and at times it was far more than this. Also, soldiers in the first two years

> The candidate's own knowledge is linked to the source evidence.

> Historical knowledge is specific here.

of the war got very little home leave back to Britain. Nevertheless, this practice of rotation kept British soldiers from having excessive periods on the front line may be one reason why morale in the British Army seems to have been higher than in the French Army, which did not do the same. Other things which improved conditions for British soldiers were the fast and reliable postal service and reasonable food rations.

British soldiers were also treated fairly well in relation to discipline and punishment. Even if the officer in source 6 is rather unreliable because, as he was an officer, Field Punishment Number One would not have been something that would have generally been applied to a person like him, the British military discipline was not that harsh during the war. Fewer than 400 soldiers were executed and nearly 90 per cent of those condemned had their sentence reduced. This suggests that military authorities were reasonably fair.

Overall, I do not think you can say that British soldiers during the First World War were entirely well looked after, as life in the trenches and the stress of fighting and seeing so much death made conditions very difficult, as source 4 and, to a limited extent, sources 5 and 6 indicate. However, the treatment of British soldiers was not as bad as it could have been in the circumstances, as soldiers did not generally have to spend extended time at the front line, as mentioned in source 5, discipline was not too excessive, and soldiers benefited from things like a reliable postal system.

Focus on the question is maintained.

40/40

The candidate gives a clear argument in response to the question and deploys the sources and their own knowledge effectively. Evidence from the sources and own knowledge are integrated in places, and conclusions are reached partially using the sources.

Reverse engineering

The best essays are based on careful plans. Read the essay and the examiner's comments and try to work out the general points of the plan used to write the essay. Once you have done this, note down the specific examples used to support each general point.

Section 4:
The impact of the First World War on the Home Front

DORA and government control

The scale of the First World War forced the government to take control of British society and the British economy to an unprecedented extent. Propaganda was used to maintain morale on the home front, and some people were directed into certain jobs, most obviously through mass conscription into the army. By the end of the war, the government was also limiting alcohol supply to try to keep workers productive, and controlling food supply through rationing.

The Defence of the Realm Act (DORA)

The Defence of the Realm Act, or DORA, was introduced on 8 August 1914. DORA gave the government far-reaching powers to decide where people worked, control industry, censor the press and control food production and supply.

Rationing

The British were heavily dependent on imports of food and fuel. By 1916 there were widespread shortages and prices rose, and consequently malnutrition became more common. The Germans' use of unrestricted submarine warfare from 1917 exacerbated the problem, as many supply ships were sunk. Hunger was a frequent occurrence among the poor in urban areas as the price of most basic foods doubled between 1915 and 1917. The government was reluctant to impose compulsory controls on food and first tried a voluntary rationing scheme in February 1917, but with continuing food supply problems compulsory rationing of some foods was introduced in 1918.

Date rationing introduced	Item rationed
October 1916	Coal
January 1918	Sugar
April 1918	Meat, butter, cheese, margarine, bacon, tea

Control of alcohol

The government introduced a number of measures to deal with the problems of drunkenness, hangovers and the perceived problem of women's drinking (which was thought to have increased during the war as some women had more independence and more money to spend).

- The Intoxicating Liquor (Temporary Restriction) Act, 31 August 1914 allowed for the restriction of opening hours in pubs.
- In June 1915, a Central Board of Control was established to restrict alcohol sales in certain areas: by 1917, 93 per cent of the public were subject to its regulations.
- Sales of beers with **chasers** and the purchase of rounds of drinks were prohibited.
- Alcoholic content of beer was reduced throughout the war and that of spirits was restricted to 70 per cent.
- The government raised alcohol duty and thus the cost of wine and beer more than tripled in price during the war whilst the cost of spirits quintupled.

These measures did reduce problems associated with drinking: in Scotland for example, the weekly conviction rate for drunkenness fell from 1,485 in 1914 to 355 in 1918. Middle class consumption of cocaine rose however, and the government introduced import controls on the drug for the first time.

Linking sources

Below are a sample part (a) exam-style question and the three sources referred to in the question. In one colour, draw links between the sources to show ways in which they agree about the effectiveness of the British government's management of the food supply during the First World War. In another colour, draw links between the sources to show ways in which they disagree.

How far do the sources suggest that the British government managed food supply effectively during the First World War? Explain your answer, using the evidence of sources 1, 2 and 3.

SOURCE 1

(From All Quiet on the Home Front *by Richard Van Emden and Steve Humphries, published in 2003. They are writing here about the problems with food supplies)*

The government was slow to react to the crisis. It was ideologically opposed to a system of compulsory rationing. In February 1917, Lord Devonport, the new Food Controller, introduced a voluntary rationing scheme. Everyone was encouraged to reduce their consumption. The aim was to shift consumption away from grain, which was predominantly imported, to meat, which was produced mostly at home… The official strategy, however, revealed a profound ignorance of the diet of working-class families, which was based on high consumption of bread. Meat, because of its expense, was a luxury. These families were the ones suffering most from increasing food prices and shortages.

SOURCE 3

(Amelia Harris, who was ten and living in London in 1917, recalls the difficulties her family had in that year)

Breakfast was tea and bread. At teatime it was bread and dripping. For dinner it was boiled potatoes. For vegetables we had cabbage leaves that we picked off the floor by the market. That was all we survived on. We were very, very poor and undernourished. For years I've been very anaemic and I think I'm suffering still from it now.

SOURCE 2

(From a letter 'to the Head of the Household' from the government's food controller urging people to cut their consumption of bread, 29 May 1917)

I wish to appeal for the immediate help of every man, woman and child in my effort to reduce the consumption of bread. We must all eat less food: especially we must all eat less bread and none of it must be wasted. The enemy is trying to take away our daily bread. He is sinking our wheat ships. If he succeeds in starving us our soldiers will have died in vain. In the interests of the country, I call upon you all to deny yourselves, and so loyally to bridge over the anxious days between now and the harvest.

Doing reliability well (a)

On page 37 are a series of definitions listing common reasons why sources are reliable or unreliable, and above are a series of sources. Explain why each source is reliable/fairly reliable/fairly unreliable or unreliable for the purpose stated, justifying your answer by reference to the definitions on page 37.

Source 1 is reliable/fairly reliable/fairly unreliable/unreliable as an account of the British government's food policies during the First World War because _____

Source 2 is reliable/fairly reliable/fairly unreliable/unreliable as evidence of the British government's food policies during the First World War because _____

Source 3 is reliable/fairly reliable/fairly unreliable/unreliable as evidence of the state of British food supplies during the First World War because _____

The creation and recruitment of a mass army

The war led to mass volunteering and later mass conscription, both of which had an important impact on British society.

The need for men

At the start of the war the BEF had 80,000 men. The size of the German Army and high British casualties during early battles, such as the First Ypres, where the BEF sustained 50,000 casualties, meant that expanding the size of the army was a priority. The **Territorial Army** was prepared for war, and the army relied increasingly on volunteers.

Recruitment to the British Army

- In August 1914, newly appointed Secretary of State for War, Lord Kitchener, predicted that he would need an army of one million men.
- On 6 August, two days after the war started, Parliament authorised the army to recruit an additional 500,000 men and this target was attained by the end of September.
- By November 1914 the recruitment of another one million soldiers had been authorised.
- The initial phase of the war saw great enthusiasm from young men to join up, and the **Pals Battalions** were very successful. One of the most famous of these was the Accrington Pals, many of whose members were killed on the first day of the Battle of the Somme.
- After the initial wave of patriotic enthusiasm dampened down, men were encouraged to enlist by means of government propaganda campaigns and pressure from others, such as employers.
- 2.5 million men volunteered for the British army during the war.
- As recruitment levels declined, Lord Derby, director general of recruiting, introduced the Derby Scheme.

The Derby Scheme

All men aged between 18 and 41 were asked to 'attest their willingness' to serve in the army if asked to do so. This encouraged some to join up, but 38 per cent of single men and 54 per cent of married men who were not working in industries considered vital to the war effort, known as **reserved occupations**, still did not sign up.

Conscription to the British Army

With the Derby Scheme by and large a failure and the army requiring even more recruits, the Military Service Act was introduced in January 1916 and all unmarried or widowed men between 18 and 41 were conscripted. In May 1916 the second Military Service Act extended this to married men. The Act did not apply to those in reserved occupations or to those who were unfit to work.

Mind map

Use the information on the opposite page to add detail to the mind map below.

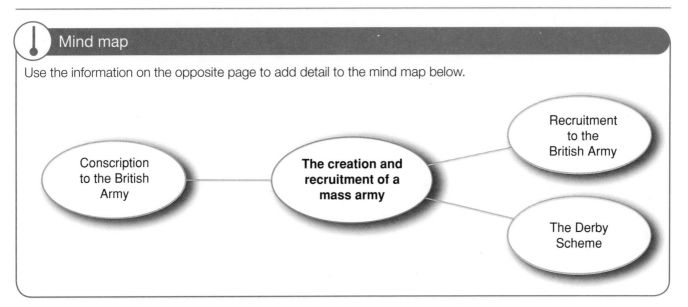

Conscription to the British Army

The creation and recruitment of a mass army

Recruitment to the British Army

The Derby Scheme

Spot the inference ⓐ

High level answers avoid summarising or paraphrasing the sources, and instead make inferences from the sources. Below is a source and a series of statements. Read the source and decide which of the statements:

- makes inferences from the source (I)
- paraphrases the source (P)
- summarises the source (S)
- cannot be justified from the source (X)

Statement	I	P	S	X
Jack Davis felt excited at the start of the war.				
Everyone in Britain felt enthusiastic about the war when it began.				
Some of those who volunteered to join the British Army at the start of the First World War were naïve about what fighting in a war involved.				
Some of those who volunteered to join the British Army at the start of the First World War felt excited at the prospect.				
The British Army had no difficulty getting people to volunteer to fight during the war.				
Conditions on the Western Front were dangerous and difficult.				

SOURCE 1

(Jack Davis recalls his feelings at the time he decided to enlist in the British Army at the start of the First World War)

I don't think people realised the seriousness of it then. We understood that we were in danger from the Kaiser and that we had to defend our territory by all means. It came as no surprise that war was declared. For me it was a bit of excitement and I thought, 'Well, might as well enlist' – 'fresh fields' and all that. I never realised then what it meant, we had no idea what we were going into. My first six months at the front were characterised by part depression and part disbelief that this could be war.

Support for and opposition to the war

For the most part, British people were supportive of the war effort, and government propaganda and newspaper coverage helped to maintain this.

Support for and opposition to the war

At the start of the war, the level of patriotic enthusiasm indicates that the British public supported the war effort. All the main newspapers and political parties were pro-war and the Trade Unions agreed to significant reductions in their rights to assist with the war effort (see page 60). As the war dragged on, however, there were some signs of opposition, such as that expressed by decorated war hero Siegfried Sassoon in 1917. The number of strikes started to rise after 1916, which may indicate that workers were less content to support the war effort: in 1918, 5.9 million working days were lost through strike action. Workers mainly protested about economic issues though, and the number of strikes remained substantially below the pre-war level.

Conscientious objectors

Conscientious objectors refused to fight in the war for reasons of religious faith (for example if they were **Quakers**), conscience or political belief (i.e. if they were **pacifists**). The No Conscription Fellowship (NCF) was established in 1914 to represent and assist those who did not want to fight. The NCF had a national network of branches by 1915 and campaigned unsuccessfully against the introduction of conscription. The NCF monitored the treatment of conscientious objectors by the government, promoted their message through their newspaper, *The Tribunal*, through their press office and through contact with MPs.

The treatment of conscientious objectors

The government established tribunals under first the Derby Scheme and later the Military Service Act to hear the cases of conscientious objectors in order to establish whether these were genuine cases of a moral or 'conscientious' objection to war. The Act allowed conscientious objectors to perform duties short of fighting in the **Non-Combatant Corps** or under the supervision of tribunals, such as the very dangerous job of stretcher bearer. The second Military Service Act allowed some to be exempted from making any kind of contribution to the war effort: 16,100 people chose to register as conscientious objectors under the terms of this Act.

Tribunals were often very unsympathetic towards conscientious objectors, and some were even sentenced to death after refusing orders to serve. The government, however, **commuted** these sentences and imprisoned or put to work those who did not want to participate in the war effort. Some agreed to do work for the **Pelham Committee**, established by the government to allocate work to conscientious objectors. Those who refused this were imprisoned and often mistreated: 73 conscientious objectors died in custody.

Around 6,300 conscientious objectors served in non-combatant roles on the Western Front and 7,750 worked for the Pelham Committee; 1,500 **absolutists** were jailed.

Public attitudes to conscientious objectors

Through propaganda, the government encouraged the public to take a negative view of conscientious objectors as lazy, unpatriotic shirkers and they were widely reviled. Un-uniformed young men were sometimes jeered at or given a white feather, denoting cowardice.

You're the examiner

Below are a sample part (a) exam-style question and two paragraphs written in answer to this question. Read the paragraphs and the mark scheme provided on page 78. Decide which level you would award the paragraphs. Write the level below, along with a justification for your choice.

How far do sources 2 and 3 support the evidence of source 1 about attitudes towards conscientious objectors? Explain your answer, using the evidence of sources 1, 2 and 3.

Sources 2 and 3 partially support the evidence of source 1 about attitudes towards conscientious objectors. Source 1 reveals that it was difficult to be a conscientious objector because the British public were so hostile and 'many were subjected to abuse and violence.' Source 3 substantiates this as Len Payne was 'pushed off his bike' when returning from a No Conscription meeting. Source 3 supports the contention of source 1 that the police were particularly hostile towards conscientious objectors: in source 1, it is said that pacifist meetings were often broken up by mobs and that this was sometimes 'with the collusion of the police.'

However, in contrast to the evidence of sources 1 and 3, the objector in source 2 receives a positive reaction: he encounters some soldiers who agree with his view that the war constitutes murder, shake him by the hand and urge him to 'stick to it matey.' This is in contrast to the 'abuse and violence' that source 1 indicates conscientious objectors might receive. Both sources 2 and 3 have some limitations as both are just depictions of one event. The sources may suggest that the attitude of soldiers was more positive than that of the general public, although the soldiers in source 2 are not necessarily typical, particularly as they are under arrest and may therefore feel angry at the British army because of that.

Level: Reason for choosing this level:

SOURCE 1

(From All Quiet on the Home Front *by Richard Van Emden and Steve Humphries, published in 2003)*

The overwhelming strength of public opinion was behind the war and it took immense courage to become a 'conchie'. Many were subjected to abuse and violence. Pacifist meetings were often broken up by mobs, sometimes with the collusion of the police.

SOURCE 2

(From an account given by a conscientious objector who was a Quaker)

It was right at the beginning that I learnt that the only people from who I could expect sympathy were soldiers and not civilians. I was waiting in the guard room when five soldiers under arrest came in. When they asked me what I was in for, I was as simple as possible 'I am a Quaker and I refused to join the Army because I think that it is murder.' 'Murder?' one of them whispered, 'it's bloody murder!' As they went away they each came up to me and shook me by the hand. 'Stick to it, matey,' they said, one after the other.

SOURCE 3

(Len Payne was a conscientious objector during the First World War. Here he recalls how he was treated)

On my way from a No Conscription meeting, I was pushed off my bike and arrested by two policemen. At the local police station, my clothes were taken from me and I slept the night on a hard board in a cell.

The war economy

During the First World War, Britain developed a **war economy**. This entailed government intervention in industrial production and the **labour market**. To try to deal with the need for manpower in some parts of the economy, army recruiting officers were told not to enlist men who worked in 'reserved occupations' such as coal mining. Some skilled workers were even returned from the trenches in order to work at home.

Although most of the British economy remained in **private ownership**, the government took control over many aspects of labour, production and prices. Profits in war industries were not permitted to exceed those of 1913.

Sector of the economy	Government action
Munitions	In response to a crisis over shortages of munitions, a Ministry of Munitions was formed in May 1915. The Ministry co-ordinated the production and prices of munitions, and the purchase and supply of the raw materials needed such as steel. By 1918, there were 3 million munitions workers in more than 20,000 factories.
Mining	Problems with labour shortages and disputes between miners and mine owners in South Wales (culminating in the huge mining strike in July 1915) resulted in the extension of government control over the region's mines.
Transport	**Rail:** Rail company managers ran the railways on behalf of the government through the Railway Executive Committee. Profits were limited to 1913 levels and troops were transported for free. **Shipping:** The government gradually took over **merchant shipping** through the war and by 1918 almost all merchant ships were under government control.
Agriculture	Huge problems with food shortages and rising prices led the government to introduce rationing and also to take measures to boost production and cultivate extra land. In 1917 the Board of Agriculture used 2.1 million extra acres of land for food production whilst Agricultural Executive Committees supervised farmers' work.

The impact of the war on workers

In March 1915, the **Trades Union Congress** (TUC) agreed with the government certain restrictions on workers' rights:

- Workers agreed not strike for the duration of the war.
- Wage increases were to be authorised by the government.
- The government could direct workers to certain jobs.
- Workers could not leave their jobs without the permission of their employer.
- Workers could not refuse to do overtime.

In return, wage rates were safeguarded, profits in war industries were limited and employers had to agree to **arbitration** in labour disputes.

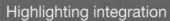
Below are a sample part (a) exam-style question and a paragraph written in answer to the question. Read the question and the answer, as well as the sources. Then, using a highlighter, highlight examples of integration – where sources are used together. You cannot reach Level 3 or Level 4 of the part (a) mark scheme (see page 78) without integration of the sources. What level would you award the paragraph?

How far do the sources suggest that British workers were supportive of the war effort during the First World War? Explain your answers, using the evidence of sources 1, 2 and 3.

All the sources indicate that British workers were supportive of the war effort, though it is revealed that there were strikes by some workers during the war. However as source 1 shows, the fact that the workers' representatives in the Trades Union movement so quickly gave up the right to strike 'without extracting anything in return' suggests strong support for the war from the labour movement and all the sources agree that British workers showed 'patriotism'. Further, the sources show that, although strikes did in fact continue, this cannot be taken as a sign that British workers did not support the war. Source 1 points out that, even at its worst, the level of strike action was significantly lower than before the war, suggesting a 'cooperative mood', while source 2 similarly makes clear that strikes were not held because soldiers were anti-war. This is substantiated by source 3 which states that Gwen Herford's father 'would rather not have struck, especially with the war on' and reveals that the strike action was probably for pay as the miners families 'were very poor'.

SOURCE 1

(From Blighty – British Society in the Era of the Great War *by Gerard De Groot, published in 1996)*

The trade unions immediately surrendered their most effective weapon – the strike – without extracting anything significant in return. The only conceivable explanation for this cooperation is simple patriotism, strengthened by a conviction that a thankful government would reward the workers when peace returned. The effects of this cooperative mood were immediately evident. At the beginning of August 1914, around 100 strikes were in progress; by month's end just 20. … Even in 1918, the worst year for industrial action, the number of days lost was 5,900,000 which compares favourably with 9,800,000 in 1913, the same in 1914, and 40,900,000 in 1912.

SOURCE 3

(Gwen Herford lived in South Wales during the First World War. Here she remembers her father's involvement in a miner's strike in 1917)

Practically all the families were very poor, like us. … Dad was a quiet, patriotic man and he would rather not have struck, especially with the war on. He supported the war, he volunteered for the army but they told him he would be more useful as a miner. He didn't go to all the meetings that the police tried to break up, but he decided to go along with the majority when they came out on strike. … I can't remember how long the coal strike lasted, but they got what they wanted.

SOURCE 2

(From a government report into strikes during the First World War)

[Strikes had] not arisen out of any desire to stop the war… On the one hand [the men] were reluctant to hold up the war to the detriment of their relatives in the trenches. On the other hand, it seemed important to them in their own interests to keep their trade privileges intact. One has an impression, in short, of unrest paralysed by patriotism.

The impact of the war on women

Women and work during the First World War

The need for servicemen led to an increase in the women's workforce of 1.6 million.

In the *transport industry*, the number of women employed in the railways increased from 12,423 in 1914 to 65,000 in 1918. Women undertook roles in areas not considered typical arenas of female employment such as signal operating. Women were also employed on buses as ticket collectors and drivers: in 1916 the London Omnibus Company aimed to train 500 women a month. In *agriculture,* the Women's Land Army (WLA) was formed in January 1917 to work in farming and forestry: 16,000 members of the WLA helped to bring in the 1918 harvest. The mainly middle- and upper-class members of the WLA were supplemented by a great many women from rural areas who also took on extra work in the countryside. In the *Civil Service* women's employment rose dramatically from 33,000 in 1911 to 102,000 in 1921: most were employed in clerical roles. Perhaps the most significant contribution that women made was in the *munitions industry*. By the end of the war the industry employed 950,000 women: 80 per cent of munitions were produced by women. This was dangerous work as workers were not properly protected from the toxic substances that they were handling.

Reactions to women's employment

Reactions to women's increased role in the labour market were often negative. Some male workers and some trades unions resisted greater female participation: tramway workers resolved in May 1915 that it was 'dangerous' and 'unwise' to employ women to work on trams. Agreement to increase female participation was often achieved on the understanding that women would leave employment after the war. Working men's resistance was not entirely down to sexism however: they rightly felt that employers sometimes preferred hiring women because they could get away with paying them less.

Women's contribution to the military

By 1918, nurses employed in military hospitals numbered 23,000. These nurses were supplemented by voluntary nurses from the War Office's Voluntary Aid Detachments to the Sick and Wounded (VADs): over the course of the war 38,000 women volunteered and worked as assistant nurses, ambulance drivers and cooks. A small number of women from the First Aid Nursing Yeomanry (the FANY) also helped at the front line with ambulance, car and truck driving. VADs and FANYs tended to be middle and upper class as they were not paid for the work that they did.

The First World War and the status of women in British society

The impact of the First World War on women was significant but can be over-stated. Parliament finally granted women the vote in October 1918 albeit on a different basis from men (women of 30 and over were granted the vote at this stage while men had only to be 21).

Women's role in the labour force increased, and women's union membership rose by 160 per cent. However, many women were forced out of jobs after the war as demobilising soldiers returned, and women's pay remained only half that of men.

Below are a sample part (b) exam-style question, the three sources referred to in the question and a paragraph written in answer to the question. The paragraph contains only a limited amount of detail. Annotate the paragraph to add additional detail to the answer.

> Do you agree with the view that the First World War significantly changed the role and status of women in British society? Explain your answer, using sources 1, 2 and 3 and your own knowledge.

Many things changed for women during the First World War. Women took jobs that previously men had done, which challenged sexist assumptions about the role of women: source 2 reveals that in Hull women were allowed in the end to become transport workers. Women also made huge contributions to the war effort through their work and this was something that some politicians thought necessitated giving women the vote, as source 1 shows. In source 1, Prime Minister Asquith shows that he thinks that there was a good case for giving women the vote saying that women 'have aided, in the most effective way, the prosecution of the war'. Women were given the vote at the end of the war, and this indicates that the war had changed their role and status, partly because of women's contribution to the war effort.

SOURCE 1

(From a speech to the House of Commons by the then Prime Minster, Herbert H Asquith on women's suffrage in 1916. Asquith had been known before the war for his opposition to votes for women but here he speaks out in favour)

What are you going to do with the women? I have received a great many representations from those who are authorised to speak for them, and I am bound to say that they presented to me not only a reasonable, but, I think, from their point of view, an unanswerable case… they point out – and we cannot possibly deny their claim – that during this War the women of this country have rendered as effective service in prosecution of the War as any other class of the community… they fill our munitions factories, they are doing the work which the men who are fighting had to perform before, they have taken their places, they are servants of the State, and they have aided, in the most effective way, the prosecution of the War.

SOURCE 2

(From Blighty – British Society in the Era of the Great War *by Gerard De Groot, published in 1996)*

Transport workers in Hull 'absolutely refused to work with women' and threatened to strike. They were not successful, but in Liverpool male dockers prevented the employment of women for the entire war. Even the cotton unions, which had a long history of women members, resisted further female incursions in the mills. Male spinners feared that if females were employed 'We shall have the employers saying there is nothing in spinning if a girl can do it, and will pay accordingly.' The worries were real because employers did actually resort to these arguments. Transport workers in Cardiff were especially resistant toward married women whose husbands were employed.

SOURCE 3

(Instructions issued to members of the Women's Land Army during the First World War)

You are doing a man's work and so you are dressed like a man; but remember that just because you wear a smock and breeches you should take care to behave like an English girl who expects chivalry* and respect from every one she meets. Noisy or ugly behaviour brings discredit, not only upon yourself but upon the uniform, and the whole Women's Land Army. When people see you pass… show them that an English girl who is working for her Country on the land is the best sort of girl.

*courteous and respectful behaviour

Propaganda and public attitudes

The press, propaganda and censorship

During the war, newspapers were used to disseminate the propaganda which the government thought was so vital to retaining public support for the war. Newspaper owners like Lords Northcliffe, Rothermere and Beaverbrook were entirely happy to fulfil this role.

The government established a secret propaganda department early on in the war and additionally the foreign office had a News Department aimed at influencing the stories about the war in the newspapers. In 1917, a Department (later Ministry) for Information was set up which included a Propaganda Section and a News Bureau, which censored press stories and issued **D-notices**. This body included an Advisory Committee containing three senior newspapermen.

War reporting

Initially war correspondents were not permitted to report from the Western Front as military authorities were concerned that their reports might damage morale. After some MPs complained about the lack of reliable news reports, an army officer, Colonel Swinton, was appointed as an official war reporter but his accounts were censored. Pressure to grant access to the front to genuine war reporters continued and, from Spring 1915, four leading correspondents were allowed to report from France.

There are various issues with the reliability of the war correspondents' accounts:

- For the most part they co-operated fully with military authorities and their reports were not therefore objective: five correspondents received **knighthoods** after the war.
- Reports often downplayed the sufferings of soldiers.

Anti-German feeling

Publications like the **John Bull** and the *Daily Mail* stirred up anti-German feeling and some German businesses in Britain were attacked. Anti-German attacks intensified after the Germans sank the ship the *Lusitania* in May 1915, drowning many of the civilian passengers aboard. The press seized on any opportunity to depict the Germans as barbaric, reporting extensively upon stories of German atrocities. Some of these were genuine incidents: the German army did respond brutally to Belgian resistance to their invasion. Some stories were, however, exaggerations or inventions, like one infamous *Times* report of April 1917 claiming that the Germans used the dead bodies of soldiers for oils and pig fodder.

Examples of German 'brutality'

Some incidents were particularly focused on by the press as examples of German brutality:

The Sinking of the Lusitania May 1915: the ship was carrying arms but the British press and public were outraged that the Germans would attack a ship carrying so many civilians.

The execution of Edith Cavell: Norfolk-born nurse Edith Cavell was shot as a spy by the Germans for helping British prisoners of war to escape: there was a national outcry in Britain.

The role of the cinema

Films about the war made up about 10 per cent of the films shown in Britain during the war: the popular film *The Battle of the Somme* (1916) recreated scenes from the battle. Newsreel footage also gave cinema audiences information about the nature of the war.

The following sources relate to the reports of the British press during the First World War. Read the guidance detailing what you need to know about the First World War. Having done this, write an exam-style part (a) question using the sources.

Study sources 1, 2 and 3.

How far do the sources suggest that

_____

_____

Explain your answer, using the evidence of sources 1, 2 and 3.

SOURCE 1

(Sydney Bond recalls the attitudes of the press and public towards the Germans during the First World War)

The fact was that every national paper, and every provincial paper, had really two centre pages entirely devoted to propaganda belittling the German and his behaviour in the war. This had an enormous effect on us all. These broadsheets began to contain deliberate propaganda, blackening the German and his attitude, brought on by the sinking of ships and the attacks on the east coast. These broadsheet had lurid details, and they hurriedly got every artist they could to draw a vivid picture. And then they sank the *Lusitania*, and that caused such a stink that it was then all full-blast propaganda, to turn the German into an absolute swine.

SOURCE 2

(From Blighty – British Society in the Era of the Great War *by Gerard De Groot, published in 1996)*

The second form of censorship was the control exercised over what journalists wrote. The pre-war practice of voluntary censorship was continued; editors submitted to the Bureau any material felt to be sensitive, but were not required to do so. The Bureau regularly issued D-notices designed to warn editors about topics they should avoid. Though some editors complained that the system was open to exploitation by the unscrupulous, self-censorship worked because the government could impose heavy penalties under DORA against those who transgressed. The most notable example was the two week-suppression of the *Globe* after it published stories in November 1915 that Kitchener was being forced to resign.

Recommended reading

- Gerard de Groot, *Blighty – British Society in the Era of the Great War* (1996), see particularly Chapter 5, 'War by improvisation: money, manpower, munitions, food', pages 79–108.

- Arthur Marwick, *The Deluge – British Society and the First World War* (1965), see Chapter 3, 'New Women', pages 117–162.

- Richard Van Emden and Steve Humphries, *All Quiet on the Home Front* (2003). Chapters 7 and 8, 'The Year of Hunger' and 'Toil and Trouble' are particularly useful for information on food supply, work and workers (pages 189–254).

SOURCE 3

(Philip Gibbs, a war correspondent who reported from the Western Front, reflects upon his work)

My dispatches tell the truth. There is not a word, I vow of conscious falsehood in them… but they do not tell all the truth. I have had to spare the feelings of the men and women who have sons and husbands still fighting in France. I have not told all there is to tell about the agonies of this war, not given in full realism the horrors that are inevitable in such fighting. It is perhaps better not to do so, here and now, although it is a moral cowardice which makes many people shut their eyes to the shambles, comforting their soul with fine phrase about the beauty of sacrifice.

Exam focus

On pages 68–71 are sample answers to the exam-style questions on this page. Read the answers and the examiner comments around them.

(a) Study sources 1, 2 and 3.

How far do the sources suggest that the work women did during the First World War improved their lives? Explain your answer using the evidence of sources 1, 2 and 3 and your own knowledge. **(20 marks)**

(b) Study sources 4, 5 and 6.

Do you agree with the view that there was strong support in Britain for fighting the First World War? Explain your answer using sources 4, 5 and 6 and your own knowledge. **(40 marks)**

SOURCE 1

(From Richard Van Emden and Steve Humphries, All Quiet on the Western Front, *published in 2003. Van Emden and Humphries are describing the situation in Britain immediately after the First World War)*

Unemployment rose dramatically and with it the criticism of working women. It was not just in munitions work that women were made redundant. In jobs not traditionally associated with females – bus conductors, railway guards or tram drivers – men were allowed to reassert their predominance. Only in clerical, secretarial and shop work, where large numbers of women had been employed before the war, were women allowed to hold on to their modest gains in the labour market.

SOURCE 2

(From an article in The Times *newspaper, published in February 1915)*

Even if many of the posts formerly held by men which women are now filling are for the duration of the war only, and will have to be yielded up should their original holder return safe and sound, they will have tested women's capacity in a way that may have a lasting effect on women's work in the future.

SOURCE 3

(An account of the work of the Women's Land Army, the WLA, from Gerard De Groot's book Blighty – Britain in the Era of the Great War, *1996)*

The work was exhausting, dangerous and dirty, with long hours, poor accommodation, strict regimentation and low pay. Most working-class women had sufficient sense to realise that money could be made more easily in cities. Lured by pastoral fantasies, a disproportionate number of middle class women did join the WLA, often giving up well-paying jobs to do so.

SOURCE 4

(Bill Moore remembers the mood in Sheffield during the First World War)

People were starting to turn against the government and against the war. In my family, it was heart-breaking. My father had just been killed. My mum had died just after I was born and I was brought up by my grandmother, my father's mother. She was devastated by my father's death. Her hair turned white in a couple of weeks. I remember watching her and my grandfather weeping, trying to console each other. And some of my uncles never came back from the war, either. That was what was happening to lots of families in Sheffield. They were exhausted and they were angry. I can only describe it as a dark cloud hanging over us. But Sheffield was a proud city that had fought for its rights, going back to the days of the French Revolution, and that's what it did again in the war. Many times the engineering factories were out on strike.

SOURCE 5

(From Gerard De Groot's Blighty – Britain in the Era of the Great War, *1996)*

Despite the prohibition against spreading dissent, political protest did not disappear. But after 1914, it was carried out mainly by fringe ideologues who maintained a lonely and futile opposition to the government. Their less committed followers took either a pragmatic or patriotic decision to support the war. The pacifists, socialists and feminists who remained were for the most part leaders without followers. They came together in the anti-war movement: pacifists because they believed war was wrong, socialists because it was a consequence of capitalism, and feminists because it was a scourge of patriarchy.

SOURCE 6

(From Richard Van Emden and Steve Humphries, All Quiet on the Home Front, *2003)*

The pacifist movement had never provided significant opposition. Its weakness was to be exposed when conscription had been extended to the many thousands of men who had no desire to be soldiers. If ever there was a time when the ground was fertile for pacifism, it was in 1917 just as war weariness set in. Yet only 16,100 men and women took advantage of a clause in the Military Service Act to register as conscientious objectors, amongst them Bertrand Russell, Fenner Brockway and Sylvia Pankhurst.

(a) Study sources 1, 2 and 3.

How far do the sources suggest that the work women did during the First World War improved their lives? Explain your answer using the evidence of sources 1, 2 and 3 and your own knowledge. **(20 marks)**

The sources suggest that the work of women during the First World War changed their lives to some extent. Source 1 and 2 reveal that women were given more job opportunities during the war, and this may have allowed some women more financial freedom, and improved the lives of women in that it reduced the prevalence of stereotypical ideas about what women were capable of. However, the sources also reveal that many of the improvements were short lived and that some of the job opportunities, such as that provided by the Women's Land Army, did not improve the lives of women.

Sources 1, 2 and 3 all show that the First World War gave women the chance to undertake a wider range of roles in the jobs market which may have improved their lives. Source 1 states that women had undertaken roles 'not traditionally associated with females — bus conductors, railway guards or tram drivers' during the war. Source 2, a report from The Times suggests that similarly the jobs done by women during the war 'have tested women's capacity', implying that sexist ideas such as women not being capable of undertaking certain jobs had been challenged by the war. The fact that a long-established newspaper like The Times is commenting on this suggests that the work that women did during the war improved attitudes towards women as the report comments approvingly on women's role during the war. Sources 2 and 3 also imply that the work that women did during the war may have improved their lives in the sense that women doing the kind of difficult work outlined in source 3 ('exhausting, dangerous and dirty' work) contributed to the positive attitude expressed towards women in source 2.

However, the sources do not entirely support the idea that the work women did in the First World War improved their lives. Source 3 reveals that some middle class women actually reduced their standard of living by taking war work, in this case on the land: this negative view contrasts with the positive impression given in source 2. It is not really possible to generalise from source 3 however, as the Women's Land Army only employed a fairly small number of middle- and upper-class women and their experiences are unlikely to have been typical. Sources 2 and 3 also show that many of the gains in the employment market that women made were short term and just for the duration of the war. The author of source 2 points out that many women will be displaced from their new jobs as soldiers return, and source 3 reveals that this did indeed occur, particularly in the areas

> Similarities between the sources are drawn out.

of work that had not traditionally employed women: in many areas of work 'men were allowed to reassert their predominance' as source 2 had predicted. Source 3 reveals that women's work during the war may have actually had a negative impact upon women's lives in the sense that immediately after the war ended, many seem to have resented women holding these jobs: this is in contrast with source 2's prediction that society would retain an admiration for the increased 'capacity' women had shown. This may perhaps indicate that source 2 cannot entirely be trusted: the newspaper may have just wanted to send out a positive message about women's work during the war in order to keep women's morale up. In that sense source 2 may be a form of propaganda.

Overall, the sources suggest that the work that women did during the First World War brought them some gains in terms of increased opportunities revealed in sources 1 and 2, and the opportunity to prove what women were capable of, as shown in source 2. However, the apparently positive view of women's capabilities that source 2 implies cannot be entirely relied upon as the source may be propaganda aimed at maintaining women's morale. Finally sources 1, 2 and 3 all suggest that in some ways the work women undertook during the war did not improve their lives as it could be difficult and dangerous, as shown in source 3 (although this source only describes a small area of women's war work), and many of the gains in the job market were quickly reversed when the war ended, as indicated in source 3.

> Useful comment on the significance of the provenance of the source.

> The sources are used as a group to address the question.

20/20

The sources are used as group to consider the issue and detailed comparisons are made. The candidate remains strongly focused upon the question throughout and reaches reasoned judgements in the conclusion.

(b) Study sources 4, 5 and 6.

Do you agree with the view that there was strong support in Britain for fighting the First World War? Explain your answer using the evidence of sources 4, 5 and 6 and your own knowledge. **(40 marks)**

There was strong support in Britain for the First World War and sources 5 and 6 show this. However, the sources all demonstrate that support for the war was not universal and that some individuals, like Bill Moore's family in source 4, and groups, such as the No Conscription Fellowship, did not support the war effort.

The question is answered straight away in the introduction providing a clear start to the essay.

Most people in Britain were strongly supportive of the war effort during the First World War. The lack of support for the position of pacifists and conscientious objectors indicates this. Sources 5 and 6 reveal that most people did not agree with the opponents of the war. Source 5 shows how small they were in number describing them as 'fringe ideologues' whose opposition to the war was 'lonely and futile'. The depiction of them as 'fringe' and 'lonely' suggests that they had no support and therefore that British people supported the war effort. Source 6 backs this up, as it reveals that only 16,100 people registered as conscientious objectors, showing that the overwhelming majority of people, even those who were reluctant to fight, did not support their position. Further, the active hostility that many conscientious objectors encountered indicates that British people were strongly in favour of fighting in the war. Pacifist meetings were often attacked, and the police usually did nothing to stop this. Young men who had not signed up were sometimes targets for abuse on the streets or were handed white feathers to imply that they were cowards, indicating that some British people were so strongly supportive of the war effort they were inclined to attack or pressurise those who might not be. Finally, source 6 suggests that support for the war was not just to be found at the start of the war but that even when 'war weariness set in', as in 1917 when the war had been dragging on for 3 years, and prices and shortages were increasing, opposition to the war was still insignificant, thus suggesting that support for the war was strong.

Sources are deployed early on in this paragraph.

However, while most people were strongly supportive of Britain fighting the First World War, this support was not universal. Source 4 shows that in Sheffield there were signs that opposition was growing as the war went on, and this evidence contrasts with that of source 6 that war weariness did not lead to an erosion of support for the war.

Bill Moore says that in his family and in Sheffield in general people were turning 'against the government and against the war' as they were 'exhausted and they were angry', partly because of the losses they had suffered. He also implies that workers in Sheffield may have been opposed to the war as there were many strikes. This source may suggest that in some areas of the country, support for the war was less than in others. However, although it is true that the number of strikes rose as the war went on, most strikes were not about opposition to the war but were just about economic issues.

Some groups and individuals were opposed to the war throughout and source 5 says that there was an 'anti-war movement' and that 'political protest did not disappear'. This source reveals that a range of people, 'pacifists, socialists and feminists' opposed the war. Similarly source 6 indicates there was a pacifist movement and that some people like Sylvia Pankhurst supported it: the No Conscription Fellowship was established early on in the war and by implication its members did not support the war as they did not want to fight. This organisation had some support as it had branches across the country. However, sources 5 and 6 do show that these organisations had very little impact: as source 6 says: 'the pacifist movement had never provided significant opposition'.

The candidate's own knowledge is used to develop and extend the point.

In conclusion, I agree that there was strong support for the fighting in the First World War in Britain, shown by the lack of support for, and indeed sometimes active hostility towards, the pacifists. Sources 5 and 6 reveal this. However not everyone supported the war, as all the sources show, and source 4 does imply that the British people may have felt less happy with fighting the war as it dragged on. Even at this point, however, according to source 5, the British still did not support ending the war: support may have been a little less enthusiastic than in the early part of the war, but it was still there.

40/40

A reasoned judgement reached which is integrated with the evidence of the sources. The candidate also develops the points from the sources with well-selected examples of their own knowledge.

What makes a good answer?

You have now considered four sample A-grade answers. Use these essays to make a bullet-pointed list of the characteristics of an A-grade essay. Use this list when planning and writing your own practice exam essays.

Glossary

absolutist in the context of the First World War: someone who refused to make any contribution at all to the war effort in Britain; i.e. they refused not only to fight but also to work as a stretcher-bearer or in other war work, etc

aide de camp assistant to a senior military officer

anaesthesia drug induced removal of pain

annexed when one country is taken over by another

arbitration resolving a dispute between two parties through the involvement of a third party

arms race a situation where a number of powers expand their military capacity as they compete to obtain dominant forces

armistice an agreement to stop fighting

artillery long-range guns that fire missiles

aristocratic of the hereditary upper class

Balkans a multi-ethnic region of south-east Europe

Belgian Flanders a part of western Belgium bordering France where much fighting took place during the First World War

BEF the British Expeditionary Force: the battle ready part of the British Army after the Boer War; the British Army in Belgium and France during the First World War

Black Week the name given to the week (10–17 December 1899) in which the British Army, who had thought that they would be able to win easily in the Boer War, suffered a series of defeats against the Boers at Stormberg, Magersfontein and Colenso. 2,776 British soldiers were killed, wounded or captured

blockhouses mini-forts that enabled British troops to have a network of military control across Boer lands

bombardment an attack by artillery

cavalry soldiers mounted on horses

commuted of a judicial sentence: reduced to a less severe penalty, e.g. death commuted to imprisonment

chaser a short alcoholic drink, usually a spirit, drunk with or 'chased' by another alcoholic drink, usually a pint of beer

chemical warfare use of weapons containing poisonous chemicals

concentration camps camps used to contain large numbers of civilians during a war. The name was also applied to the Nazi camps used during the 1930s to contain the opponents of Nazism

court martial a disciplinary court of the armed forces

creeping barrage an attack by a group of soldiers who are protected as they advance by a arc of artillery fire landing ahead of them

D-notices warnings issued by the government to newspapers requesting that they do not report on certain items on national security grounds

entrenched something that is long established and hard to shift

fettered tied up/restrained with chains or manacles

gangrene death or decomposition of body tissue caused by infection or problems with blood supply

guerrilla campaign/guerrilla warfare unconventional warfare commonly used by inferior forces against better equipped armies. Guerrilla fighters hide and launch surprise attacks. Sabotage is also a common tactic. Guerrillas may use civilian areas to conceal weapons

haemorrhage substantial bleeding

Hindenburg Line a German system of defences in north-west France built 1916–1917

iconic relating to something that is famous and thought to represent a particular idea

imperial relating to an empire

imperialism the policy and idea of pursing the creation and maintenance of an empire. Imperialism also relates to the ideas that might be used to justify such a policy

infantry foot soldiers

Irish nationalists supporters of a fully independent Irish state

John Bull a nationalistic British publication

knighthood an honorary title given by the British monarch

labour market a situation in which workers compete for jobs and employers compete for workers

landslide in the context of an election: an overwhelming victory

left-wing a term used to describe political beliefs and movements that seek to create a more equal society

merchant shipping civilian ships that carry passengers or goods

meritocratic a system whereby people achieve advancement or promotion due to their abilities

'Methods of barbarism' the name given to a speech by Liberal leader Henry Campbell Bannerman condemning British use of concentration camps during the Boer War

mines explosive devices

ministering angel a term applied to a person who comforts and helps another

mobilise prepare an army or country for war

musket a type of gun

nepotism giving favour or promotion to a family member or someone close to you

neutralised of an area: removed from any one country's control

neutrality with respect to a country: a position of remaining unaligned in international affairs and out of international conflicts. Alliances and engagement in wars are avoided

no man's land the land between two entrenched armies in the First World War

Non-Combatant Corps established in 1916, a part of the British army that did not fight but contributed to the military effort

Orthodox Christianity a type of Christianity found in Eastern Europe and Russia

Ottoman Empire an Istanbul-controlled empire that lasted from the 13th century to the 20th century

over the top phrase used during the First World War to describe the action whereby soldiers launched an attack from their trenches towards their opponents' trenches

pacifist one who believes that war is wrong in all circumstances

Pals Battalions battalions formed of friends or colleagues who volunteered together

Pelham Committee a government-appointed committee that tried to find war work for conscientious objectors during the First World War

physiological relating to the body

pro-Boer the hostile name given by supporters of the Boer War to those who opposed it

provenance the origins of something; usually in history this relates to the origins of a historical source, i.e. who produced the source, when, where and why

private ownership the ownership of capital or property by private individuals or private companies

psychological relating to the mind

purchase of commission the practice in the British Army of obtaining a promoted position by paying for it

Quakers a religious group with Christian roots who emphasise spiritual experience rather than religious doctrine. Pacifism is a key part of Quaker belief

relief the end of a siege (e.g. of Ladysmith, Kimberley and Mafeking)

reserved occupations those jobs that were deemed during the First World War to be of such importance to the war effort that the men who worked in these areas were exempt from army service

reserve forces sections of an army where soldiers combine other work with army training in peacetime (e.g. the Territorial Army in Britain). Reserve forces can be called upon to serve full time during times of war

revisionist (in a historical context) a historian who seeks to challenge established interpretations

Schlieffen Plan the German war plan before the First World War. The plan was to avoid the possibility of fighting Russia and France simultaneously by defeating France in the time it would take the Russian Army to mobilise (thought to be six weeks)

septicaemia blood poisoning

scorched earth policy a military tactic involving the destruction of the homes, settlements and agricultural land of the enemy

shells explosive projectiles fired from artillery

shell shock psychological condition caused by prolonged exposure to warfare

shrapnel a shell that explodes into pieces in the air

Spion Kop site of a famous battle of the Boer War on 23–24 January 1900. Spion Kop was the hill on which the battle was fought. The British suffered defeat despite outnumbering the Boers. 243 British soldiers were killed and 1,250 wounded or captured

stalemate in warfare, a situation where neither side makes substantial gains over a period of time

suffrage the vote

telegraph an electrical system for transmitting simple messages via wires

Territorial Army an unpaid volunteer reserve force of the British Army

Trades Union Congress a national organisation representing British trades unions

trench foot a painful foot condition caused by prolonged exposure to cold and damp conditions

trench fever a fever transmitted by lice

typhus, typhoid, dysentery, cholera diseases acquired by contact with contaminated food or water

Uitlanders the name give by Boers to non-Boer Europeans living in Boer lands

unrestricted submarine warfare attacks by submarines on all shipping including supply ships, passenger ships and, in the case of German attacks during the First World War, US ships heading to Britain

war economy an economy organised primarily to win a war

war of attrition a prolonged conflict in which each side is gradually worn down

Timeline

1854 British and French involvement in the Crimean War begins

The battle of Alma

Start of the Siege of Sevastopol

The battle of Balaclava including the incidents of the Thin Red Line and the Charge of the Light Brigade

Florence Nightingale arrives in Scutari

1855 A cold winter

The Sanitary Commission arrive

Mary Seacole's British hotel opens

The end of the Siege of Sevastopol

1856 The Treaty of Paris ends the Crimean War

Establishment of the Victoria Cross

1870–71 The Cardwell Army Reforms

1899 The start of the Second Boer War

The sieges of Ladysmith, Kimberley and Mafeking commence

Black Week

1900 Spion Kop

The relief of Mafeking

British victories in Johannesburg and Pretoria

The start of the Boer guerrilla campaign

Start of use by the British of concentration camps and scorched earth policies

1901 Emily Hobhouse's reports on concentration camps appear

Henry Campbell Bannerman makes his 'Methods of barbarism' speech condemning British methods

The Fawcett Commission confirm Hobhouse's finding

1902 The Peace of Vereeniging ends the Boer War

1906 Local authorities allowed to provide free school meals

1907 Medical check-ups for school children introduced

1911 Part 1 of the National Insurance Act introduced compulsory health insurance for poorer workers

1914 Archduke Franz Ferdinand assassinated

Start of the First World War

DORA introduced

The Race to the Sea

Massive expansion of the British Army authorised

1915 Ministry of Munitions established

1916 The Military Service Acts allow conscription of first single and then married men

The Battle of the Somme

1917 The USA joins the war

The Battle of Third Ypres/Passchendaele

Department for Information formed

1918 Rationing of some food introduced

The Germans' Spring offensive

German advance halted at Amiens

German defeat

Answers

Section 1: The impact of the Crimean War

Page 5, Spot the inference

The British and the French won the Battle of Alma. (X)

The Russian Army suffered high casualties at Alma. (I)

British and French tactics were very successful during the Crimean War. (X)

Russian soldiers were in a dreadful state following the Battle of Alma. (S)

Some wounded Russian soldiers asked for water after the Battle of Alma. (P)

Page 9, Highlighting integration

The first answer is of a higher level.

Page 9, Explain the difference: suggested answer

Source 1, a poem on the Charge of the Light Brigade by Tennyson, gives a dramatic account of the Charge which glorifies the soldiers. This differs from the more factual account given in sources 2 and 3, which are the views of two historians. Source 1 is likely to be more dramatic as it is a poem, whilst the historians are likely to want to give a more factual and measured account. Additionally, Tennyson was writing in the immediate aftermath of the Charge, and this may explain his desire to glorify the soldiers. As a British subject, he may also have felt patriotic towards them whereas the historians may have a more objective view.

Page 11, Write the question: suggested answer

Use sources 1 and 2 and your own knowledge.

Do you agree with the view that Mary Seacole made a greater contribution to assisting British soldiers during that Crimean War than Florence Nightingale?

Explain your answer, using sources 1 and 2 and your own knowledge.

Page 13, Doing reliability well: suggested answer

Source 1 is reliable as evidence of problems with organisation within the British army during the Crimean War because the author, as a historian, is an expert on the subject.

Source 2 is unreliable as evidence of the qualities of the leadership of the British Army during the Crimean War because the author is writing in order to promote the Earl of Cardigan's reputation and does not therefore given an objective account.

Page 15, Develop the detail: suggested answer

The Crimean War did result in significant reforms to the British Army **which made the army more efficient, more meritocratic and more accountable**. As Source 1 says, the structure of Army Organisation was simplified **and brought under the responsibility of one department, the War Office, as part of the Cardwell Army Reforms of 1870–1871.** Therefore hopefully the problems of inefficiency that had occurred during the Crimean War, **for example with respect to the distribution of supplies from Balaclava Harbour,** would be resolved. Source 1 explains 'duplication of responsibility for military finance and supply had been largely erased'. This reform was significant because during the Crimean War there were too many different organisations, **eleven in total,** involved in trying to supply and fund the army. **The Cardwell Reforms also introduced** significant reforms to the British Army during the Crimean War in the area of purchase of commission: **this practice was abolished and promotion would now be through merit. Additionally, flogging in peacetime was abolished, and the Commander in Chief of the army was made accountable to Parliament through the Secretary of War.**

Section 2: The impact of the Boer War

Page 23, Write the question: suggested answer

Use sources 1, 2 and 3 and your own knowledge.

Do you agree with the view that the British public was completely supportive of the war effort during the Boer War?

Explain your answer using sources 1, 2 and 3 and your own knowledge.

Page 25, Write the question: suggested answer

Use sources 1, 2 and 3 and your own knowledge.

Do you agree with the view that the British public was very supportive of British participation in the Boer War?

Explain your answer, using sources 1, 2 and 3 and your own knowledge.

Page 27, You're the examiner

This paragraph should be awarded high Level 4 as there is sustained focus upon the question, sources are compared in detail and provenance is considered.

Page 29, Highlighting integration

The first answer is of a higher level.

Page 31, Develop the detail: suggested answer

I agree that the Boer War led to significant reforms in Britain. One area that was reformed was the British Army. As source 1 says, the Esher Report made recommendations to improve the army after the Boer War. **The Esher Report led the army to adopt more clearly defined roles, such as chief of the general staff, and to improve professionalism in the British Army through, for example, better training facilities.** The source shows how important these were as it says that without the Esher Report 'it is inconceivable that the mammoth British military efforts in two world wars could have been possible, let alone so generally successful'. The Haldane Reforms were also important changes within the army that happened after the Boer War, as source 2 indicates. This source, an extract from the Reforms themselves, shows that after the Boer War the army was reformed in an important way with the formation of a 'field force... completely organised as to be ready in all respects for mobilisation immediately on the outbreak of a great war'. **The Haldane Reforms introduced this crucial force, the BEF, which was to prove so important at the start of the First World War. The Reforms also established the Territorial Army.** This was to be important during the First World War. In addition, the Boer War led to significant reforms to social welfare **because the war had highlighted the poor physical condition of many in Britain.** As source 3 says, free school meals and medical services for children were introduced **in 1906 and 1907. National Insurance was also provided for the poorest workers from 1911.**

Section 3: The impact of the First World War on the Western Front

Page 37, Doing reliability well

Source 1 is fairly reliable as evidence of the mood in Britain at the start of the First World War because it is a first-hand account and therefore reflects the author's actual experiences. However as it is only one person's story it is not completely reliable as it only provides a partial account. In addition, the author may have misremembered details.

Page 39, Eliminate irrelevance

The British Army were fairly well-equipped during the First World War. Source 2 supports this as even though the soldier is describing horrible trench conditions he says that 'winter clothing had been issued'. ~~Trenches were established from early on in the war.~~ This clothing sounds good quality as it included leather fur jerkins and lined gloves. Later on in the war, the British also received steel hats which protected them from injury. ~~British soldiers suffered hundreds of thousands of injuries during the First World War.~~ The British Army were also well-equipped in that they increasingly had good weapons like grenades and the Vickers machine gun. Source 1 indicates that the British army had sufficient weaponry as it reveals that, despite reports in *The Times* to the contrary (which are described in the source as 'misleading'), high explosive shells were in fact available, as Asquith had told munitions workers.

Page 43, Spot the inference

In September 1918 the British Army advanced quickly. (I)

The Third Ypres was not worth the cost of fighting it for the British. (source 1 X, source 2, I)

British commanders were highly effective by 1917. (X)

General Ludendorff felt stressed in 1918. (P)

The British Army had some success in exhausting the Germans in 1917. (I)

British successes in 1918 were entirely down to the weakness of the Germans (X)

Page 43, Write the question: suggested answer

Use sources 1, 2 and 3 and your own knowledge.

Do you agree with the view that the British Army had considerable military success during 1917–1918?

Explain your answer, using sources 1, 2 and 3 and your own knowledge.

Page 45, Highlighting integration

The paragraph is of level 4 standard.

Section 4: The impact of the First World War on the Home Front

Page 55, Doing reliability well

Source 1 is reliable as an account of the British government's food policies during the First World War because the authors, who are historians, are experts on the subject.

Source 2 is fairly reliable as evidence of the British government's food policies during the First World War because the author, the government's food controller, was presumably an expert on the government's food policy. However, the source is not totally reliable because as the controller is a representative of the government, his letter may to some extent be propaganda.

Source 3 is fairly reliable as evidence of the state of British food supplies during the First World War because it is a first-hand account and therefore reflects the author's actual experiences. However as it is only one person's story it is not completely reliable as it only provides a partial account. In addition, the author may have misremembered details.

Page 57, Spot the inference

Jack Davis felt excited at the start of the war. (P)

Everyone in Britain felt enthusiastic about the war when it began. (X)

Some of those who volunteered to join the British Army at the start of the First World War were naïve about what fighting in a war involved. (I)

Some of those who volunteered to join the British Army at the start of the First World War felt excited at the prospect. (I)

The British Army had no difficulty getting people to volunteer to fight during the war. (X)

Conditions on the Western Front were dangerous and difficult. (I)

Page 59, You're the examiner

These paragraphs should be awarded high Level 4 as there is sustained focus upon the question, sources are compared in detail and provenance is considered.

Page 61, Highlighting integration

The paragraph is of level 4 standard.

Page 63, Develop the detail: suggested answer

Many things changed for women during the First World War. Women took jobs that previously men had done which challenged sexist assumptions about the role of women: source 2 reveals that in Hull women were allowed in the end to become transport workers. **Similarly women worked as bus drivers and ticket collectors on London buses from 1916.** Women also made huge contributions to the war effort through their work, **as munitions workers for example: 80 per cent of munitions for the war were produced by women** and this was something that some politicians thought necessitated giving women the vote, as source 1 shows. In source 1, Prime Minister Asquith shows that he thinks that there was a good case for giving women the vote saying that women 'have aided, in the most effective way, the prosecution of the war'. Women were given the vote at the end of the war, and this indicates that the war had changed their role and status, partly because of women's contribution to the war effort.

Page 65, Write the question: suggested answer

Study sources 1, 2 and 3.

How far do the sources suggest that the British press produced reliable reports on the First World War during the period 1914–1918?

Explain your answer, using the evidence of sources 1, 2 and 3.

Mark scheme

For some of the activities in the book it will be useful to refer to the mark scheme for
the unit. Below is the mark scheme for unit 2.

Part (a)

Level	Marks	Description	
1	1–5	• Selects relevant material from the sources. • No attempt to compare the sources. **Level 1 answers are highly simplistic.**	• Sources are copied or paraphrased.
2	6–10	• Selects relevant material from the sources. • Notes similarities and differences between the sources. **Level 2 answers have some focus on the question, but significant weaknesses. For example, comparisons may be superficial or the answer may demonstrate some misunderstanding of the sources.**	• Simple conclusions about provenance.
3	11–15	• Selects relevant information from the sources. • Detailed comparison of similarities and differences. **Level 3 answers address the question and demonstrate a good understanding of how the sources agree and differ.**	• Begins to use provenance to explain similarities and differences between accounts. • Begins to answer 'how far…?'
4	16–20	• Selects relevant information from the sources. • Detailed comparison of similarities and differences. **Level 4 answers clearly answer the question and demonstrate a sophisticated understanding of the evidence of the sources in their historical context.**	• Provenance is used to explain similarities and differences between accounts and to weigh the evidence. • Sustained focus on 'how far…?'

Part (b)

AO1: Using historical knowledge to form an explanation

1	1–6	• General points with limited focus on the question. • Inaccurate supporting evidence. • No integration of sources and own knowledge.
2	7–12	• General points with some focus on the question. • Accurate and relevant – but generalised – supporting evidence. • Attempts integration of sources and own knowledge.
3	13–18	• General points with secure focus on the question. • Mostly accurate and relevant supporting evidence. • Some integration of sources and own knowledge.
4	19–24	• General points with strong focus on the question. • Accurate and relevant supporting evidence. • Integration of sources and own knowledge.

AO2: Analysing source material

1	1–4	• Copied or paraphrased information from the sources. • Little focus on the question.
2	5–8	• Summarised information from the sources and used to provide a simple answer to the question.
3	9–12	• Evidence from the sources is selected to support and challenge the view expressed in the question.
4	13–16	• As Level 3. • Weighs the evidence of the sources and uses this in reaching an overall judgement.